SO…YOU WANNA BUY A CAR

SO...YOU WANNA BUY A CAR

Insider tips for saving money and your sanity

Bruce Fuller
Tony Whitney

Self-Counsel Press
(a division of)
International Self-Counsel Press Ltd.

Printed in Canada

First edition: April 1997

Canadian Cataloguing in Publication Data

Fuller, Bruce, 1942
    So — you wanna buy a car

    (Self-counsel series)
    Includes bibliographical references
    ISBN 1-55180-061-6

    1. Automobiles — Purchasing. 2. Selling — Automobiles.
I. Whitney, Tony. II. Title. III. Series.
TL162.F84 1997   629.222′029′7   C96-910881-1

The advertisement reproduced on page 15 is reprinted with the permission of Ford Motor Company of Canada, Limited.

The advertisements reproduced on pages 40 and 105 are reprinted with the permission of General Motors of Canada Limited.

The advertisements reproduced on pages 50 and 85 are reprinted with the permission of Chrysler Canada Ltd.

Cartoons © 1997 Bruce Fuller.

Self-Counsel Press
(a division of)
International Self-Counsel Press Ltd.

1481 Charlotte Road	1704 N. State Street
North Vancouver, British Columbia	Bellingham, Washington
V7J 1H1	98225

With much love to my parents, who afforded my brother and me great adventures on the road, but who unfortunately would drive and drive and drive and drive and drive until everyone in the car had to go to the bathroom at the same time.

And to Todd, Chantal, Nadine, and Lauren, who I'll stop for whenever they want.

And to my Karen, in her never-ending search for the scratchless, dent-free car that she never, ever has to fix.

B.F.

To my older boy Robin, who'll really need this book one day soon.

And to my car-nut youngest Spencer, who probably won't.

And to my mother who is always pleased to see my name on a book, even if it's not the great novel I've always planned.

T.W.

CONTENTS

FIGURES

WORKSHEETS

ACKNOWLEDGMENTS

Of the very limited number of books we were able to find on car buying, one really jumped out in front of the chromed grille and shone brighter in the headlights: *Everything Women Always Wanted To Know About Cars*, by Seattle-based author, Lesley Hazleton. Published by Doubleday, Lesley's book is easy to read, well illustrated, and hilarious in a lot of places. We very much appreciate Lesley's permission to quote from her book.

We gratefully acknowledge the quiet support of the Chrysler Corporation, General Motors, and the Ford Motor Company for their assistance and kindness in pointing us in a lot of the right directions, for providing us with terrific advice that works no matter which manufacturer you wish to deal with, and for their permission to use some terrific golden-oldie ads to shake memories loose for our older readers.

And to our publisher, Self-Counsel Press, who is making it possible for you to save a fortune on buying a car. If you want to.

INTRODUCTION

Take thousands of well-worked and burnished
bits of metal:

> *Engineer them*
> *Weld them.*

Fold in multi-hued hunks of molded plastic.
Twist in a mile or so of wire. Combine with
glass, nylon components, hard and soft rubber
shapes. Stir in computers with their host of
abilities and memory chips. Sprinkle with
optional exotic leathers and a few choice exotic
woods (for presentation purposes and just the right
"nose"). Add requisite safety features and a
generous helping of durability for years of service.
Toss together with a good measure of
riding-in-comfort luxury and a stereo system.
Let dozens of chefs stir the broth. (What you
say? ...too many chefs spoil it?) Let move through a
factory kitchen in mere hours. Ship while still hot to
a showroom near you. Shine up and sell.

THE CAR.

What a great treat for all of us. A marvelous concoction for transportation and other things. A truly magnificent recipe!

It turns us loose, gets us over there, then back here. It takes us to school, the office, the shop, the factory, cousin Jenny's, Brad's birthday party, and grandma's house for Thanksgiving. To your girlfriend's place and your boyfriend's pad, and to the take-out, drive-in, or favorite lookout. To the lumber store, grocery store, dry cleaner's, movie theater. To the lake, the seaside, or up the mountainside.

And to the insurance office, the gas station, the tire store, that battery place, the muffler shop ... and to the auto dealership for another one.

a. AND SO *YOU* WANNA BUY A CAR?

We hope this book will help you a long way down the road to becoming a satisfied car owner. If the car you're thinking about is your first, the information between the covers of this book will better prepare you to become a more informed and wiser purchaser come buying time, at that moment of truth behind closed doors ... with The Closer.

If you're already a car owner and this is your second purchase (or third, or ninth), perhaps our comments will add to your acquired-the-hard-way wisdom and help move you into the driver's seat of that special new vehicle with a bigger smile on your face than last time round.

And talking about smiles ... there's simply no reason why you can't approach the whole challenge of buying a car as fun. Our approach to writing this book was to have a good time looking at, learning about, and driving what's out there, and while we've collected some serious thoughts for your consideration, we'll be presenting most of them with a grin.

One of us (Bruce) just plain likes cars and thinks that driving should be an enjoyable, hassle-free, yet exciting way to get from A to B and that making the purchase shouldn't be a chore or a pain in the butt if you're dealing with the right sort of seller.

The other of us (Tony) knows a helluva lot about what really makes cars work, how they should work for you, and what you should expect when you're looking for something that suits your needs.

The world of car-buying is not so mysterious or complicated when you understand what's involved and who's involved and mix and match all that with your own unique, highly personal needs. We enjoyed pulling together a whole lot of little bits you'll need to know to make wise choices when it comes time for one of life's bigger buying decisions.

We've combined our car-buying, car-using attitudes in a non-academic, readable style that's ideal for your own use or for passing on to anyone who cares about making THE BIG DECISION: buying a car.

But what do we know about it? Well, let's go back to the beginning.

b. OUR VERY FIRST CARS

1. Bruce's '31 Hupmobile

Walking across the dusty yard toward the barn, I heard a metallic, clinking sound. The sliding door was open a bit and I saw the farmer under his tractor in the beam of sunlight. Looking up, he nodded a hello and continued draining oil from the crankcase.

I launched into the sales pitch with a well-rehearsed, "Was just in the neighborhood talking to folks about the paper and wondered if you'd like a free subscription?" I couldn't help but notice something with spoked wheels showing under a tarp over in the corner.

"Got no money, son, but might give it a try if you buy that there car I got for sale." He grinned. "It's a Hupmobile, a '31 Hupmobile … was my Dad's. Haven't driven 'er for about five years. Bought a half-ton that does us jus' fine."

Brakes worked okay. Wipers too. No flats. "Battery's shot though. If you want, we can start 'er with the tractor. If you like 'er I'll make you a helluva deal … and I'll have my boy take yer company car there back to town first thing tomorrow."

A half hour later he was waving goodbye with my $205 clenched tightly in his fist ($5 for a well-traveled tractor battery and my $200 travel expense advance for the Hupmobile). What a deal! I had just bought my first car! My first ever car! (Plus he had signed up for that free one-month subscription.)

The car looked great sitting in the driveway below my apartment. It started easily enough (until it rained, that is) and edged up and down the driveway to the wonderment of my neighbors and friends … but I couldn't afford the insurance or operating expenses. Two of the tires went flat the day after I got home. "Your brakeshoes *(what?)* are probably all dried out and that's why they don't work so well. And Bruce, did you ever notice that right front fender is coming loose?"

So I patched the flat tires (they had real inner tubes, like a mountain bike), and with some body-filler I bought at a hardware store I shored up the loose fender. I sanded and varnished the wooden-spoked wheels and, with a burst of energy, blackened the sidewalls to fill in and smooth out their weathered cracks. A little elbow grease and paste wax buffed the exterior to an impressive glow. Chrome polish for the trim with just a touch of silver paint to camouflage the peeled parts.

The Hupmobile remained in the driveway until I put the *For Sale* sign under the windshield wipers late Friday night. Saturday morning it was sold — for $1,000. Wow! I was in the used-car business.

Since those days I've bought, sold, leased, cabbed, rented, borrowed, been chauffeured-in, tried-out, or tested a few hundred cars, trucks and vans, a tractor, and an old workhorse Cat. I've toured Toyota's humungous plant in Nagoya, Japan, and the neighboring, robot-controlled, just-in-time parts warehouse. I've had tea with the sheet metal guys at Peter Morgan's little Morgan factory outside London, England, where I bought a $75 wiring harness to secrete home wrapped in dirty shirts. "Looks like stuff for a sports car," the customs official said, "but let's say it's for a tractor so I won't hafta charge you duty."

"…no kidding, it's a wiring harness for my tractor!"

For years I owned a classic Morgan until it was snapped away during a bitter divorce. Took the kids for a Big Mac in a '51 Bentley; slid our Jag XJ12 coupe into a snow-filled ditch heading to ski country; had three little ragtop Beetles, Chryslers, Pontiacs, Oldsmobiles, and Buicks of various types and vintages, Chevys, Fords, and a peppy Triumph convertible that went straight down the highway but always looked like it was heading left (previously in a wreck, but a really good deal). I drove a girlfriend's bug-eyed Sprite until a tree jumped out and whacked me, and I butted bumpers in city traffic as a part-time cabbie piloting umpteen brands of taxis on their last, no-sir-these-shocks-ain't-busted legs (yup, trunk lids held down with coat hangers and bungee cords).

Bruce: *The beautifully lacquered, burled oak, flip-down tables built into the back of the front seat seemed perfect for lunch on the way to the Saturday movies. The kids and I got our burgers to go and picknicked in the luxurious leather-cushioned rear compartment. "Is this what the Queen does at McDonald's?" my daughter, Chantal, asked.*

I worked for a company that had an automotive division. They gave me company cars to use. "We take cars from our new car dealership, put 'em through our lease guys, and make used cars outta them. Then we bring 'em back and make money all over again" said the boss.

Never once have I had advice on what to buy. What to get. I've flown by the seat of my pants, emotionally sucked into the vortex of I-can't-wait-to-have-it.

Now my friend Tony, he's a whole lot different from me.

He's a mechanical guy. He's a race car, test track, take-it-to-the-red-line kind of guy. He's driven every major course in the world and at neck-snapper speeds most of us only read about. He has sat at drawing boards analyzing running speed-safety ratios, and his rainy driveway has a different-car-a-day look to it. He's an honest-to-goodness, no-bull auto specialist, reporting through his syndicated columns and television series on the latest airbags allowable, gadget gizmo giveaways, and best bang-for-the-buck buys.

2. Tony's Morris Minor convertible

My first automotive pride and joy was a used (but very clean, as they say) 1959 Morris Minor convertible. Even back then, automotive critics were describing it as "*adequate* rather than *exceptional*."

You don't get much in the way of driving dynamics with a Minor, but to me it was the coolest thing on wheels. When the very awkward top was folded, it was fun to drive and be seen in, even if it fell well short of being a true sports car.

Sitting behind the sprung steering wheel (ever seen one of those?), I would imagine myself piloting a D-type Jag at LeMans — and let's face it, a Morris Minor at 70 mph *feels* like it's going as fast as a D-type at LeMans!

It was gun-metal gray (same as James Bond's Bentley and Aston Marton, I kept reminding myself) with red leather seats, no less. Quite soon after I bought it (from a girlfriend's brother-in-law who would now be called a "curber"), I was rear-ended by a Jag that came off much worse than the Minor. The bumper was dented and I never did replace it . . . so for the rest of my ownership the Morris sported a racy, bumper-less look from the rear.

I drove the thing half way across Europe and it never gave a moment's trouble, though there were a few times when its notoriously unreliable electric fuel pump would need a good whack to keep it working.

When I emigrated to North America and became prosperous enough to buy a new car, the first one off the lot was a bright red, 1970 Ford Cortina GT Mark II . . . imported from England just like me. It was a great car. Peppy, agile, and nicely built (now what does that really mean?). Its touch of luxury was a real wood dashboard panel. No sticky-back vinyl anywhere! Cortina GTs had quite a performance image in Britain and were raced with some good success, but they really didn't cut it in a land prowled by 302 Boss Mustangs and Hemi Barracudas.

Since those early driving days, my auto writing career has taken me from a pretend race driver in that Morris Minor to the cockpits and front seats of some pretty exotic equipment and around the best-known international Grand Prix circuits in the world. I've evaluated hundreds of cars, vans, and trucks. Driven everything from Kenworth 18-wheelers to forklifts.

Most people say that however many cars they've owned, they always remember their first with the most affection. I've always felt that way about the Morris, though the Cortina has to come in a close second.

c. HOW CAN WE HELP YOU?

You should guess by now that we both are crazy about cars and have spent a lot of time driving them and finding out as much as possible about them. Between us we hope to pass on enough information and enough of our experiences to let you make an informed purchase (or lease or whatever) of some kind, or to help you move that older beast out of your backyard before they tow it.

But first a few words on our methods.

Throughout the book, in most instances when we are referring to vehicles of any sort, we say "cars" rather than jumping back and forth describing trucks, vans, minivans, sport utility vehicles, station wagons, or sports cars. Just replace the car-word with whatever type or model of vehicle you're thinking about, and our comments should still work for you.

We've also decided not to comment on specific models or manufacturers. In fact, from here on we rarely mention a manufacturer by name, and never as a recommendation. We want you to make your own choices when it comes to buying or selling a car. We can tell you what to watch for, how to find the best deals, and how to pay for your purchase, but you've got to take that knowledge and decide what kind of car you need.

Our one word of advice: stick with the name-brand cars and dealers. We believe that to survive and prosper in the automotive industry today, manufacturers and dealers must earn their credibility in the marketplace. Those with well-established reputations have done so.

You are who they must convince to keep going forward into the new model year. It is, after all, *you* they must please. (Keep this in mind when it's time to negotiate that buy.)

If you're heading into the world of "previously enjoyed" used cars, you'll have to pay attention to more than your gut feeling. The old saw "buyer beware" is something to keep in mind. But if you're prepared to do some reading and chatting it up beforehand, you can be reasonably sure you'll be getting into the driver's seat without too many horror shows.

Although we have both been into cars for some time now (car payments forever, it seems), *you* are about to make a very important decision, and, like everything else, timing is everything. Is it time for you to buy a car? Do you want to? Let's see.

1

WHY BUY A CAR ANYWAY?

Determining your needs

A secular sanctuary for the individual, his shrine to the self, his mobile Walden Pond.

Edward McDonagh *on the car*

Ahhh … the sheer pleasure, the complete freedom of it all!

In this shrinking world it's difficult to imagine anything that gives you more personal independence or getaway freedom than a car. Okay, maybe a horse, a boat, a plane, a pair of cross-country skis, a bike, or inline skates … but none of them compares in terms of overall practicality. In fact, chances are you'll need a car to get to your horse, the boat, the plane, the ski area, the more scenic biking trails, or that just-paved roller path around the park.

And besides, EVERYONE LOVES CARS.

Or maybe not.

Even if we don't "love" cars per se, we must agree that many people do value their ability to have a car on their own terms, and certainly they like the freedom it affords.

And whether we like cars a little or love them a lot, our lives are somehow twisted together with them in some mad way or other.

1

After divorcing the four-door sedan,
Nadine found a little sports car she really loved.

We push toy cars across the carpet before we can walk. Nearly every child "has a car"; gender has nothing to do with it. They're as mixed up in Lauren's Barbie-box as they are with the cap pistols and cowboy hat under Todd's bed.

> **Bruce:** *I bought this kid's pedal-powered, cream-colored beetle convertible. Todd was way too small to play with it, but it looked fantastic strapped to the back of our full-size cream-colored beetle convertible like it had just hatched ... or whatever beetles do.*

We get to ride in a lot of real cars over the years: snuggled and securely strapped into car seats in the earlier months; a little later, chattering with family and friends or fighting and making rude noises in the back seat; "up front" with parents on those special occasions.

Wow, great! Where the action is! Up front you get to steer. To go fast and go slow. To slow down and to stop fast. To skid on purpose. To turn right and turn left. To beep the horn. To change the radio station. To put in your own cassette. To choose the perfect CD. To turn up the heat. To adjust the air. To open the window and lean out on your elbow. To boss around the passengers.

And to go where you wanna!

And then into teenagerhood (also known as the "gotta getta car" years). "Everybody else has one — howcum I don't?" you say. Seems that cars are nearly everywhere when you're at that pre-driving test age … everywhere but where *you* want one to be: in *your* driveway.

And what about sexy stuff in a car?

a. SO WHY DO YOU NEED A CAR ANYWAY?

Here are a few reasons we came up with, and a few spaces to write in your own thoughts:

- Basic, no-nonsense transportation to and from some-place

- To take somebody somewhere (as in providing a service to your friends and family)

- To move "things"

Bruce: *I moved my office three times in that little Morgan. When the top came down it was like a tiny truck.*

- To show people you're a somebody and extend your personality

- To create and project a certain image

- To go places for fun

4

- To go places for business reasons
- To pick up girls
- To pick up boys
- To make yourself feel better about things
- To have your own space
- To not have to depend on others
- To go horseback riding, boating, flying, skiing, biking, rollerblading (among other things)
- To be free
- _____
- _____
- _____
- _____
- _____

> *I remember everything about the day I bought my first car .... I remember the day so clearly because while men take for granted the independence that cars bring, women do not. Our own car means freedom. It means control of our own lives. It means, in short, far more to us than it does to men.*
>
> *~from* Everything Women Always Wanted To Know About Cars *by Lesley Hazleton*

The basic reason most people want to buy a car is simply to get around. To get somewhere at their own convenience, when they want to get where they want to go. No schedules, no planning required. On their own terms. At their own pace.

Believe it or not, many, many people still choose not to own a car and can handle most of the above-listed reasons and requirements quite nicely, thank you very much. They cab-it, bus-it, tram-it, streetcar-it, subway-it, rapid transit-it, car pool-it, bike-it, skate-it, walk-it. In some places they horse-it, paddle-it, ski-it, skidoo-it, or dogsled-it. Some just thumb-it.

And of course some folks just rent when they need to check off anything on the list above.

> **Tony:** *Driving in southern Ireland once, I stopped in a village and asked an oldtimer whether there was a place to stop for coffee in the next town — about three miles away. The old gent replied that although he'd lived in the village all his life, he'd never been to the town down the road.*

> **Bruce:** *My son Todd and his wife decided early on in their relationship to focus on establishing home and business ownerships first and opted out of the car buying, equipping, repairing, maintaining, parking, insuring, gassing-up commitments many of their friends became enslaved to.*
>
> *Chantal, my eldest daughter, maintained her financial sanity and ability to service student loans through university by directing all her hard-earned waitressing cash flow toward the completion of a degree.*
>
> *And Nadine, another daughter, with Terry in her life who magically builds cars from the pavement up, helped him do just that, picking an assortment of valuable cast-off bits from wrecking yards, want ads, friends, and dumpsters. Yup, they've done it twice; passed safety checks, then set out on a coast-to-coast tour in that green Honda you might've seen loaded skyward with camping gear or that VW van groaning over the Continental Divide.*

b. ASK YOURSELF "WHY?"

Our advice if you're thinking about first-time car ownership: *ask yourself "Why?"*

1. Need a car for getting to work?

If this is the only reason you need a car, then ask yourself another series of questions ...

- Is public transportation available? Is it convenient for me?

- Can I share someone else's transportation? Can I carpool?

- Can I bike? Can I walk?

- Do the logistics of getting to work mean I will need a special type of car — big, small?

- When I get to work, what about parking? Is it available, affordable, safe?

- Could someone share my costs by traveling with me?

- Will I be using this for pleasure too? (If yes, consider the questions in section **3.** as well.)

2. Need a car for business?

If your needs are solely for business purposes (and if the tax people agree) you will be looking at satisfying an additional set of questions ...

- What sort of business am I in? (Is image important?)

- Do I need storage space for samples?

- Should I consider a van or truck?

- Do I need to drive clients around?

- Will my car be a portable office with cellular phone and/or fax?

- What are the budgetary limitations dictated by the tax people?

- Will I be putting a lot of mileage and wear and tear on the car?

- Should I lease or buy?

- Does my company give car allowances?

- Will I need special insurance coverage?

3. Need a car for pleasure only?

This is where you can really let your personality shine through. Or maybe your budget. Ask yourself …

- Do I want a cool car that will turn heads downtown?

- Do I want something I can use on weekends to head off into the bush for camping trips?

- Will I be driving friends around or just one special friend or just myself?

- Will I be carrying a lot of equipment or can I go for a subcompact?

- Do I really need a car or can I get around by foot, by bike, or by transit with the occasional car rental?

4. Need a family car?

Not too many years ago, the family car was a big, comfy four-door job (maybe a two-door if you were worried the kids would fling themselves onto the sidewalk to grab a puppy). Then the designers added kid-proof locks and windows that only went down an inch or two. Then along came station wagons, the ultimate family car, and now we have the larger sport utility vehicles and, of course, the minivans.

Designers really listened to the moms and dads on the latest generation of minivans. They included built-in kiddie seats with all the safety stuff, baby bottle holders (for pop cans and sometimes adjustable for the fattest coffee cups too), air conditioning, lighting and music systems, plus multiple-door, walk-through features. Today's minivans are the ultimate family cars … if you like minivans.

You can certainly still get the family car of years ago in the form of that big sedan, with the latest in comfort fittings, but you'd better be sure you have a full understanding of the kids' "latest" lifestyle needs, or those weekend outings are sure to turn into drawn out whining.

So the family car is out there in many forms — you just have to decide what you mean by "family" and then list the requirements and go shopping. When you zero in on what looks good to you, let the family try it out and get their comments.

5. Need to up-size your car?

The car you start out with is rarely the car you stay with. Your situation changes: singles get married, marrieds have families, and families have special interests and needs. Additionally, manufacturers introduce vehicles every model season with many new features, some of them convenience related, others providing the latest in safety devices. Your questions might include . . .

- Should we move from a two-door model to a four-door?

- Will we be traveling away a lot? What do we take so we have space?

- What are our lifestyle requirements? Do we need four-wheel drive? Top down? Room for bikes or for camping gear?

- Who else in the family is going to be driving?

Figure #1 shows you the cars to consider based on your needs.

Women talk differently about cars than men. Since we come newer to cars — we've only started buying cars in proportion to our numbers in the last two decades — we come without all the clutter of what we're supposed to say about them … Here are the main differences. They don't apply to all women or to all men, of course, but they do represent a very distinct trend.

Women	Men
See cars as an integral part of their lives	*See cars as machines*
Focus on reliability	*Focus on power*
Are honest and forthright when they talk about cars	*Feel they have to pretend to know all about cars*
Know more about cars than they think	*Know less about cars than they think*
Are serious about cars but also have a sense of humor about them	*Are too serious about cars, can't allow themselves to be funny about them*
Are more pragmatic about cars	*Are more image-conscious*
Think of cars in terms of a relationship (which might be why they have a sense of humor about them)	*Think of cars in terms of a romance (which might be why they have no sense of humor about them)*
Talk cars by their experience in them: what happened in and around them, people and places	*Talk cars by the numbers: cylinders, horsepower, 0-60 mph, all that tech talk*
Take great pride in ownership	*Tend to take ownership for granted*
See cars as symbols of freedom and independence	*Tend to see cars as status symbols*

~from Everything Women Always Wanted To Know About Cars *by Lesley Hazleton*

Once you feel comfortable objectively listing your realistic needs, take a look at the kinds of cars that are available and pick out a vehicle to best serve your purposes (see Figure #1 and chapter 2), set a budget that includes all expected costs (see chapters 3 and 4), then get going and . . . GO BUY THAT CAR!

FIGURE #1
CAR NEEDS

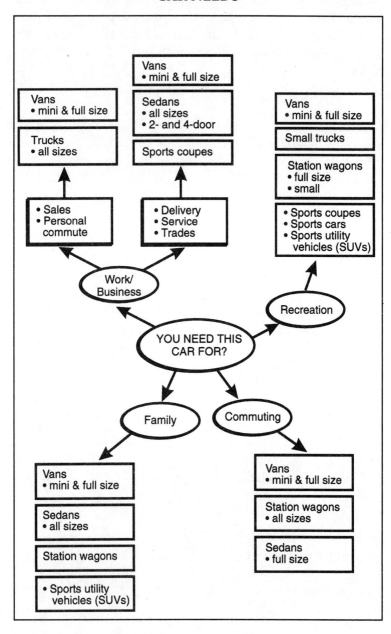

2

WHAT TYPE OF CAR?

Choosing the right vehicle

Never buy what you do not want because it is cheap; it will be dear to you.

Thomas Jefferson

If you need a refrigerator, you don't buy a picnic cooler, right?

Making the right buying decision is fairly easy with most purchases we make in our day-to-day life. It's easy to choose clothes or groceries, for instance; the world of computers might be getting a little complicated; but, cars …

In the complex and often confusing world of personal transportation, all too many people make choices that are way off the mark. Unable to separate real needs from emotional factors, unthinking auto buyers end up with vehicles they spend years struggling to live with. Yes, often within days of making their purchase and driving off the lot, they start a love-hate relationship that could've been prevented with a little planning.

When the decision is made to buy a vehicle, careful analysis of real needs and requirements is essential in the quest for automotive bliss. In other words, you should take the time to establish exactly what your transportation needs are. Are they a —

- Sedan?

- Sports coupe?

- Station wagon?

- Sports car?

- Minivan?

- Full-size van?

- Sport utility vehicle?

- Pickup truck?

The menu is varied, the choice is yours.

Following are brief descriptions of the main car types on the market today. Which type will fill your needs as determined by the questions in chapter 1?

a. SEDANS

If you need a car, the choice is usually between a four-door sedan and a two-door sports coupe. If you frequently carry passengers in the rear seats for either business or family reasons, a four-door sedan should be at the top of your list. Rear doors make access easy, and even small sedans tend to have a reasonable amount of rear legroom. (A good test for rear legroom: get in the front seat and position it for your personal driving comfort. With the front seat in this position, get into the back seat directly behind. Are your knees touching your nose? Your eyeballs? Or are they comfortably positioned for a long drive in the countryside?)

Even though load carrying might not be a major consideration for sedan buyers, it's worth seeking out a model with rear-seat backs that fold forward to extend the trunk space. Many sedans have a 50/50 or 40/60 folding seatback split, leaving you some passenger space in the back when you thread a pair of skis or a stack of two-by-fours from the trunk space to the passenger compartment.

Load up and keep
farm hauling costs down!

MOVE IT WITH → **MERCURY** TRUCKS FOR LESS!

There's a Mercury Truck built to suit a wide range of hauling jobs on your farm. The Series M-350 Light Duty model shown above is suitable for fast handling of bulky loads. Wide tread and set back front axle gives short turning—easier handling in the fields.

Mercury's "World Famous" 106 Hp. V-8—one of seven great V-8's is this year's expanded Mercury line—operates at low running cost to overcome rough off-the-road conditions all seasons of the year.

There's space for three big men in the comfortable cab. Wide non-sag seat and seat back are independently adjustable. New vinyl upholstery looks smart, is durable and easy to clean. Mercury Trucks help farmers get more work done at lower cost. Enquire about trading-in your old truck on a new Mercury model.

See or phone your Mercury Truck Dealer for catalogues with full details about new Mercury Trucks.

SEE YOUR MERCURY TRUCK DEALER

You can make a considerable change to your car's storage capability by adding a roof-mounted carrier of some kind. There are a number of good rack manufacturers making practical systems that can quickly increase the amount of usable space you have available to carry stuff. All of a sudden, that little sedan which is the only car you can barely afford — the one that's too little for anyone but you and a close friend and a duffle of gear — is reconfigured to carry canoes, kayaks, bikes, skis, and those amazing enclosed luggage carriers that look like alien pods. Check around and buy the best system you can possibly afford. Keep in mind that you can move the better ones from car to car to car and add wonderful new gizmos to carry your ever-growing inventory of recreational playthings and work toys.

Bruce: *On a family camping trip, the old coupe loaded to the heavens, we took the corner a little fast and sailed into a stump-covered field. The Chevy was a complete write-off. Soon, piled into a tow truck, we journeyed to town.*

As we passed the first car dealership, dad zeroed-in on a big green sedan. "Pull over," he told the tow truck driver.

"How much for that one?" he asked. "Will this roof rack fit? If it does, we'll take it. Okay kids, let's load up."

I'm not sure he even asked the price or discussed it with mom, but a couple of hours later we were at the campsite, unpacking gear from that roof rack fastened tightly to our shiny, new Pontiac.

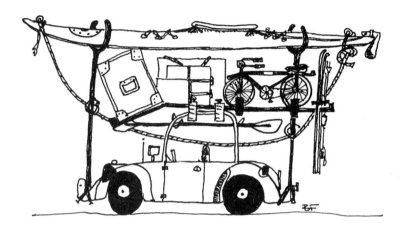

*With his little car now custom fitted with the latest in roof-rack systems,
Art is now ready for an afternoon of high adventure!*

b. SPORTS COUPES

Sports coupes are easy on the eye and boast sparkling performance, but usually offer poor accommodation and minimal visibility from the back. Back-seat passengers must struggle past a tangle of seat belts, only to find themselves scrunched up in the tiny rear compartment staring at the side window pillar. Headroom can also be a problem in cars designed mainly to look good and house two people up front. Frankly, the back seat of the average sports coupe is a good place to toss your squash bag and not much more — though there are one or two exceptions.

Some young parents like the idea of a back seat without doors for younger children to experiment with, but then mom and dad must bend, twist, and shout to secure their children firmly in car seats or seat belts. Not pretty sights or sounds on a steamy July afternoon in Atlanta.

If you rarely carry rear-seat passengers, a coupe might be a good choice. The doors are usually a little wider than the front ones of a sedan, making access somewhat easier for both driver and passenger, so a coupe is often a good choice for older folks. As well, hatchback coupes sometimes provide more luggage room than sedans with tiny trunks and rear-seat backs that don't fold.

c. STATION WAGONS

If cargo space is a major consideration, think about buying a station wagon. Though the selection is becoming restricted these days as manufacturers concentrate on vans for those who need ample room, wagons still exist and might suit your purposes very well. Station wagons continue to have a role to play and can be the ideal compromise for people who don't want the bulk and fuel thirst of the average minivan. Even smaller wagons can be surprisingly efficient load-carriers with their folding seats and easy-access tailgates. They are also easy to park and usually offer excellent visibility.

d. SPORTS CARS

Out-and-out sports cars are not a good choice for people who want some level of practicality. They are expensive to insure, appeal to thieves, are easily noticed by your local "finest," and are notorious for their poor fuel economy.

On the other hand, thousands of drivers are happy to forfeit practicality for the style and "fun content" offered by sports models — especially convertibles. Full four-seat convertibles are a rare breed, but they are around. Often these models have limited trunk room because that space is sacrificed for storage of the soft top (and frame and rear window and the little motor that tucks it all into place).

e. MINIVANS

For sheer passenger-carrying capability, there's nothing to match today's generation of minivans. Most minivans have seven seats and substantial load-carrying capacity behind the back row. As well, the back two rows of seats are often easy to remove if you need to convert your minivan into a capable cargo carrier.

The newest convenience offered minivan buyers is an extra sliding door on the driver's side. This is a huge benefit and most people who have tried one find it difficult to go back to a single rear sliding door. Expect all new minivans to have this extra door — either as a standard feature or an option.

Minivans are certainly nothing at all like the vans of old, those converted delivery vehicles with windows cut into the sides and seats bolted to the flooring. They can now be equipped to very high levels of luxury and convenience, from basic to fine leather, and the list of passenger comfort amenities gets longer and longer with each model release. Some models even offer all-wheel drive.

Manufacturers have made huge efforts in recent years to make their vans more car-like: they are agile in tight parking spaces, nimble on the freeway, and just about all of them will fit into a standard garage. Even so, vans are still not as easy to park as cars — especially smaller cars — and some of them find it difficult to pass a gas station without turning in.

These factors, plus the fairly high prices for fully equipped models, tend to put minivans quite low on the wish lists of first-time vehicle buyers.

f. FULL-SIZE VANS

North America's "big three" auto manufacturers still offer full-size vans, but these seem to have become the domain of buyers who need maximum capacity for large families or for business purposes. Available in multiseat configurations or in panel van mode for commercial users, they are a less viable proposition than minivans for first-timers.

g. SPORT UTILITY VEHICLES (SUVs)

Sport utility vehicles (SUVs) and light trucks are the hottest selling segments of the auto market right now.

A typical SUV has a boxy, practical shape with room for up to five passengers, greater-than-usual cargo capacity, and four-wheel drive (4WD) for go-anywhere capability. The category covers everything from compact import units and domestic off-roaders right up to huge multipassenger rigs based on full-size pickup trucks. For most buyers, the choice falls somewhere in the middle and the smaller models make excellent first-time vehicles.

Since the average SUV spends less than 5% of its driving life off-road (according to automotive industry studies), the popularity of these vehicles is difficult to figure as they are not as fuel efficient and easy to drive and park as compact cars. But popular they are and manufacturers happily record better sales figures each year. Just about every maker has at least one SUV in its lineup and some offer products that cover the entire gamut from compacts to biggies.

Novice buyers with a yen for an SUV should carefully assess what they want the vehicle for. If you make regular treks out to the boonies for camping, fishing, or hunting, a "full-house" SUV with 4WD might be the only choice. The same applies if you live in a region with long and snowy winters or in an area that demands everyday travel on un-paved roads.

If, like most buyers, you live in an urban environment and rarely hit the rough stuff, it might be smart to save some cash by opting for a basic two-wheel drive (2WD) SUV if you must have one. A simplified two-door, 2WD rig is often priced thousands of dollars lower than its fully optioned counterpart.

Similar rules apply to engine choices. Today's SUVs can be had with anything from thrifty four-cylinder powerplants right up to huge and powerful V-8s. If the vehicle you have your heart set on is offered with a choice of engines, don't throw money away on the biggest unit available unless you plan to tow a boat or large travel trailer. For most applications, the smaller engines will get the job done just fine.

> **Tony:** *Competition is tough between car manufacturers. When I visited the Land-Rover stand at an international auto show not long ago, I was told by an executive that they'd just caught a Japanese auto industry "researcher" cutting pieces of interior fabric from one of their vehicles with his Swiss Army knife.*

h. PICKUP TRUCKS

The pickup truck market is also booming right now and, as with SUVs, not every buyer needs the huge range of optional features most manufacturers offer. While many buyers choose pickups because the demands of work give them no other option, other drivers regard them as sports vehicles and rarely use the cargo box for anything more demanding than snowboards, surfboards, or mountain bikes.

Pickups come in full-size and compact versions, and there are a couple of products that fall in between. Buyers can choose from a bewildering array of cab configurations, box sizes, drivetrains, and luxury packages. It's possible to load up a pickup with options like V-8 or even V-10 engines, leather seats, power everything, and a custom paint job — for a substantial price. Alternatively, "work special" versions have vinyl seats, rubber floor mats, and a stripped-down list of options — but cost much less.

Where powerplants are concerned, the same advice offered to SUV buyers applies. If you don't plan to haul or tow substantial loads, opt for a smaller engine. A state-of-the-art V-6 will provide more than enough power for most needs, even if you go for a full-size pickup. For compacts, many four-cylinder engines offer a lot of power and worthwhile fuel economy.

While most standard-cab pickups come with a bench seat with room for three, increasing numbers of buyers are choosing extended cab versions. Extended cabs have comfortable seating room for as many as six passengers, and even the smaller rigs will take four with ease. Just about all pickup makers offer this configuration and it is often the best choice for buyers wanting to combine workaday practicality with people-carrying capability. The rear seating area usually converts to a secure load-carrying space, thanks to cleverly folding seats.

Manufacturers and aftermarket firms offer countless accessories for pickups, but one of the most useful by far is the bed-liner, a molded plastic unit that fits into the "bed" or box of the truck and protects it from scratches, dents, and other damage. Even a load of gravel will do no harm at all to one of these useful extras, and you'll get more than your money back when it's time to trade in or sell your truck. People who use their trucks for work and need a secure place to carry tools can buy or build a custom-made box that fits in the bed and doesn't take too much load space.

The matrix in Figure #2 shows you most everything you'll need to think about when it comes to picking out your new-to-you car. We'll cover other sections of the matrix in later chapters, but first let's talk about money. Specifically, what you're going to spend on your car.

FIGURE #2
YOUR CAR — CONSIDERATIONS

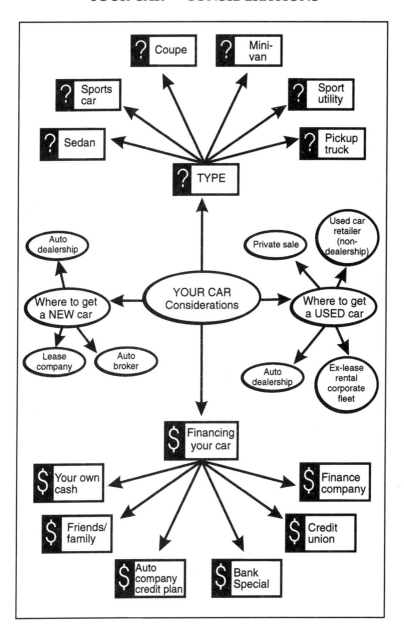

23

3

SO WHAT WILL YOU HAVE TO SPEND?

Car buying economics

An invention that makes people go fast and money faster.
The automobile according to Jimmy Lyons

As anyone with the slightest experience knows, car ownership can be one of life's most rewarding experiences or the greatest money pit yet devised.

Of course, no product that wears out over a period of time and burns quantities of increasingly more expensive fuel can ever be anything but a financial burden, but are there ways of lessening the penalty of car ownership?

Yes! It means doing your homework before you go in to the dealership. It also means budgeting for all the extra costs — such as finance charges (see chapter 4), insurance, parking, and maintenance — so that you don't pay for your car and then find you don't have enough money to run it. You can pencil in your fixed costs and the estimated costs for different cars on Worksheet #1 to determine which model fits your budget best.

Get a good idea of exactly what you want to spend as early as you can and stick to it. This is useful ammunition when bargaining with a dealer or used car vendor. Stating firmly what your limit is will often persuade the seller to close the deal, rather than coax you upmarket.

WORKSHEET #1
ESTABLISHING YOUR CAR BUDGET

ITEM	CAR 1	CAR 2	CAR 3
Name/model of car			
The car itself			
Options			
Taxes			
Cost of your money (interest on loan)			
Depreciation			
License			
Environmental permits			
Insurance			
Parking			
Operating costs:			
Gas			
Oil			
Antifreeze			
Windshield washer fluids			
Tuneups			
Tires			
Brakes			
Clutch			
Water pump			
Alternator			
Shock absorbers			
Mufflers			
Cleaning/wash/wax			
TOTAL			

a. CHOOSING A MODEL

For most people, the road to becoming a financially shrewd car buyer must start well before a trip to the dealership. As we emphasized in the last two chapters, make sure you know what kind of car meets your needs and concentrate on that sector of the market.

1. Read the write-ups

A look through the automotive press will tell the tale. Check out the glossy monthly car magazines. Many of these publish test summaries of various new models. These are worth studying if they cover the class of vehicle you are interested in.

Auto enthusiast magazines, consumer report publications, and automobile association literature are all good sources of information on vehicle reliability (we've listed a selection of widely available publications in our bibliography). Many of the magazines feature annual editions that include owner surveys, providing a good indication of how people feel about their cars in terms of reliability, general satisfaction, maintenance costs, and repeat buying. There are also annual stand-alone publications covering every car, van, and truck marketed in North America.

Browsing in a couple of issues of your local classified automobile advertising tabloid can also give you some pointers about reliability, durability, and price.

If you're already looking ahead to the day when you sell your car, the best model to buy is one that's hard to find in any type of car-for-sale publication. Good cars that are economical to run and stay the distance mechanically and cosmetically are usually passed on to relatives and don't turn up on the used car market. Try to find a bargain-priced, late model, low mileage Toyota Corolla and you'll see what we mean.

The same logic holds if you're planning to hang onto the car. A model that has held its price or that is hard to find on the used market could be a good new-car buy.

2. Visit the dealers

After you've done a little reading and have a sense of what's out there, drop by a few dealers for some window shopping. Make it clear to any salespeople who approach you that you are just looking and not planning to buy at this point. They may be persistent, but stick to your guns.

Don't be persuaded to buy the first model you take a shine to. Visit as many dealers as possible in your area and examine every model that competes with the one you have in the back of your mind — new or used. Try not to establish a preconceived idea of which model you fancy. List your basic needs and price range and keep an open mind. You may find exactly what you need at a dealership or from a manufacturer you never considered.

b. WHY DO CARS COST WHAT THEY DO?

Although cars seem expensive today, they have not really increased in price that much compared to average incomes. Given the technical sophistication of modern automobiles, they are actually cheaper than they were a few years ago. Prices reflect high manufacturing costs associated with safety equipment like air bags, crash-resistant bumpers, better brakes, and other features considered essential these days.

Today's auto industry is so competitive that manufacturers pare prices to the bone and dealer markups are slim. Often a dealer's chance to make money on a car deal comes when he or she is trying to sell you options and extras rather than the car itself. This is particularly the case if you're buying at the low end of the market. You *will* pay more for a prestige nameplate or for a low-volume specialty sports car.

One note on options: Don't waste money on extras you can do without. On the other hand, when it comes time to sell, you'll get a better price — or sell your car faster — if you selected the right options. Some, such as air-conditioning or a sunroof, can help get you a better deal when you eventually sell or trade in, although you should bear in mind that air-conditioning will use more gas when in use and may be subject to a special tax in some areas of North America. Money spent on marginal options or those of a cosmetic nature — for example, two-tone paint, spoilers, fog lights, tinted windows, and other dress-up items — doesn't have much effect on reducing depreciation and is often hard to recoup at trade-in time.

*Ever so slowly Tony lowered himself though the
optional sunroof. "What a terrific extra!" he thought.*

> *Tony: Sometimes options prove to be a good buy for reasons you might not expect. I once locked the keys in my car while it was parked on a busy street with the engine running. To make things worse, it was pouring rain and there was almost no fuel in the tank. I got in by forcing (and damaging) the sunroof.*

If you are looking at two very similar cars and one sports a higher price tag, that one probably has extra standard equipment, more safety features, and a higher potential re-sale value due to its maker's reliability record.

1. What about buying used?

If the car you want doesn't fall within your budget as a new model, think about buying a used one (we talk about buying used cars privately in chapter 6) or a "demonstrator" that may only have a few thousand miles on its odometer (see section **2.** below).

If you do decide to buy used, you will want to study the used car reports in the automotive and consumer magazines and annuals listed in the bibliography. Some of these rate used cars on the basis of owner surveys and other simply log the number of complaints they get about a specific model.

The number of owner complaints is not always a good indication of used car reliability. If the model sells in huge quantities, a few dozen complaints are just a drop in the bucket (unless you happen to be one of the unlucky few!).

Publications that rate owner satisfaction and list repair costs give a better indication of what might be a good used car buy. It's not a bad idea for a first-time buyer to look for something that will be cheaper to fix when the inevitable problems occur.

Every year the automotive fraternity (not the manufac-turers, but auto clubs, consumer groups, auto publications, etc.) take a good look at those vehicles that have stood the test of time and hard use, and present a "used car performance award." If you're wondering what makes really make it, ask a dealer for a copy of the latest results published.

Remember when setting your can-I-really-afford-this-car? budget (see Worksheet #1) to compare apples to apples as best you can. You'll be surprised when the "bottom line" figures show you that the higher initial cost of a new car might actually work out to less than the cost of a used one when you add in the used parts that will soon need to be repaired or replaced. Many new car manufacturers offer excellent long-term warranty and extended maintenance programs so your new car upkeep costs can be much lower than the upkeep costs for your "less expensive" used car.

2. Demonstrators

Traditionally, a demonstrator, or "demo," is a car that has been used by a dealership for demonstration purposes. The car you'll test drive with the dealership's salesperson is a demo. Demos, executive cars, and media testers are usually sold through dealerships when they reach a certain mileage, usually around 7,500 miles (12,000 km) or so.

These cars can be a great buy. They usually come on the market in the fall, when cars for the next model year are arriving. If you're shopping for a new car, check to see if there are any demos of the model you want. Such a car will cost quite a bit less than the new model but should be in good condition, still carrying an extensive warranty, and with any minor bugs fixed up to keep it fit for driving.

b. WHAT ELSE WILL YOU HAVE TO PAY?

1. Licenses and permits

Find out what license fees and other costs of driving you must pay in your area. In some locations, a special sales tax or permit tax might be levied for older models that are not as environmentally friendly (i.e., those that do not have specific anti-pollution features). Factor these costs in when you are figuring out the price you'll have to pay for a new car.

Also consider your parking costs. Monthly parking rates can be high in some major cities, especially if you live in an apartment or work downtown.

2. You'll need insurance

Insurance is an expense that all drivers have to bear and there isn't much that can be done to reduce this — other than opting for a more docile car than the high-performance sports car you may have had in mind. Most insurance rates are reasonable enough if you think about it.

If you happen to be a 21-year-old NHL star, a rookie pitcher for the Yankees, or a teenage tennis ace who cleaned the women's singles court at Wimbledon (with a couple of speeding tickets under your belt) looking to insure a new 'vette, you'll be facing a premium that matches the sticker price of an economy hatchback. Of course, with today's sports salaries, it'll be spare change for you.

If you're a 53-year-old bookkeeper tooling around in a Chevy Cavalier with nary a ticket to your record, however, chances are the premium won't be much more than the price of a weekend in a decent hotel.

Shop around. The insurance industry offers many kinds of packages and there are deals to be put together. There are also payment plans that can fit into most personal budget schemes.

A haunting specter for all car owners is the possibility (yes, on the increase) of having your new pride and joy scooped up from under you. Some cars are much more appreciated by thieves, more "theft-worthy," than others, and many people like to take this into account when buying. Believe it or not, many people who can afford higher-end cars are "dressing down" and opting for basic transportation that doesn't draw attention to itself and doesn't attract a hefty insurance premium.

A recent survey indicated that the Chevy Caprice station wagon was the least stolen vehicle in North America. Topping the list of "gotta-haves" for today's with-it sleazeball crook: Ford Mustang, Chevrolet Camaro, and Pontiac Firebird. Generally, mass-produced domestic cars have components that are easily sold when they are broken up for parts, as is often the case. The best advice here is to buy a car with a good alarm system or have your dealer install a decent aftermarket unit. There are vehicles available with a variety of theft-prevention devices built in, and certainly you should consider them.

After all, not everyone wants to drive a Caprice wagon.

3. Can you afford maintenance costs?

Prospective maintenance costs are always worrying to a new car buyer, but there *are* ways of getting an indication of the kind of expenses which might lie down the road.

Check consumer publications and the automotive press to find out which cars have a tendency to break down and which ones seem to last forever. Keep the various models' reliability and sturdiness in mind as you visit dealerships and pick the car of your dreams.

Once a certain model is decided on, take the time for a brief walk from the dealer's showroom through to the service department, and ask a few simple questions before signing the deal — and the check. It's not easy to tear yourself away from that shiny new car, but the trouble is well justified.

Incidentally, owner manuals that come with all new cars and usually accompany used models give details of how often your car should be serviced. Stick to this routine and your car will maintain its worth. The auto industry is working toward more infrequent maintenance intervals — some new cars don't need a full tune-up until they've done 60,000 miles (100,000 km) — and the "sealed engine," which makes backyard tinkering impossible, is not far off.

Inquire about the cost of regular servicing to keep your selected car in good working order. Ask about basic repair jobs: how much will you pay for a set of front brake pads, a water pump, a new clutch, or an alternator? In some cases these costs can be very steep indeed and could prompt a look at another model altogether. In general, parts cost more for imports than for domestic products, but there are no hard and fast rules.

Tony: *During a widespread shortage of replacement windshield wipers in Russia, it was not unusual to see people dining with a pair of wipers removed from their car set alongside their cutlery. Many motorists found it easier to steal the essential items rather than wait months for spares to arrive.*

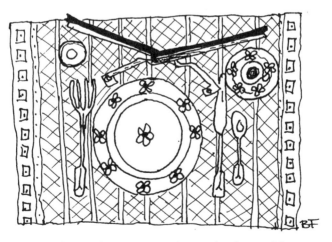

The regular Russian restaurant place setting for one driver... knife, fork, spoon, windshield wipers.

Like anything else, maintenance costs vary. You'll find some repair shops have specials at certain times of the year, while others offer amazing discounts if you decide to give them your steady business.

When repairs *are* needed, ask the shop to use manufacturer's parts. There's no point skimping by using low-cost counterfeit parts from offshore sources. These can be unreliable and may have a shorter lifespan than the items they replace … meaning you'll have to pay to replace them that much sooner.

> **Bruce:** *Every now and then the gas pedal seemed to stick, and I had to get my big toe under the edge of it and pull up or risk ramming someone in front of me. I phoned a couple of other people I knew with old Morgans and followed their unanimous suggestion: "Get a screen door spring from any hardware store."*
>
> *"Haven't sold one of these for a screen door in years … we only sell 'em to Morgan owners," the clerk commented, adding, "Just cut 'er in half and bend the end to make a hook. Works like a damn I'm told."*

4. Depreciation

One other sometimes forgotten cost is depreciation. You should consider this if you plan to trade in or sell your car in a couple of years.

Even the best of cars depreciate, unless you happen to be investing in a well-restored or restorable classic (see chapter 7), but some depreciate much more frighteningly than others. Cars depreciate because they gradually wear out, even if they're carefully maintained. Also, every model is replaced by another sooner or later, and older, dated styles lose their value.

It's a good idea to study the auto market (i.e., buy-and-sell publications or newspaper classified ads) to assess how the models you've short-listed are doing by the time they're a few years old. Check out the average price of a four-year-old model similar to the one you're planning to buy new and the results can be alarming — especially in the luxury sector. Can it possibly be that the shiny status symbol you've had your eye on can drop $20,000 to $30,000 in so short a time? Sadly, it can.

You can lessen its impact by looking after your car, maintaining it, and servicing it regularly. If you plan to keep your car for many years, your actual depreciation costs will be reduced since they are spread over a long period of time. (It's still a good idea to keep the car in good shape!)

Now that you know what kind of money you need to spend, you can worry about how you'll get that money. We cover various ways to deal with car payments in the next chapter, and then you're ready to head down to the dealership.

4

SO WHERE DO YOU GET THE MONEY?

Financing your car

[Credit is] the only enduring testimonial to man's confidence in man.

James Blish

Now you know the approximate amount you want to spend, so you look at your bank balance and ....

Financing is probably the most daunting problem facing most first-time car buyers, but if a few simple steps are taken, it shouldn't be too worrisome.

Car loans are big, big business for the banks, automakers' credit divisions, trust companies, credit unions, large and small finance companies ... and loan sharks. (We won't cover the sharks in this book 'cause we feel you'll uncover plenty of them on your own.) Mom or dad, a sibling, best buddy, your boss, your boyfriend or girlfriend can all be hit up if you're close enough and you've been able to sell your needs. That might be a bit harder if you've just started a job as the office junior and you'd like a little financial first aid so you can get that snappy two-seater ragtop that'll blow the doors off everyone else's.

If you're reasonably creditworthy, you've got a good chance of getting wheels under you via one of those no-money-down, easy-payment plans you see advertised everywhere.

If you're just out of bankruptcy or a tougher-than-usual time, you'll probably still be able to find a couple of legitimate financial organizations in most centers that'll give you a second shot. After all, they own the car until you've sent that last payment, so they can always come and scoop it if you default too seriously.

While auto loans are available from many sources, you may simply want to talk to your own bank or credit union and arrange things. Or if you're buying a new or used car from an established dealership, you may prefer to take advantage of its "in-house" scheme. Dealers either use a car manufacturer's credit division or sell the contract to a financial institution. There's nothing shady about the latter, as few dealers have the financial wherewithal to carry credit paper on their own.

Incidentally, the term "OAC" that you see in tiny print in virtually every dealer's car ads, including those on TV and even billboards (and that you hear on radio ads), means "On Approved Credit." Any lender will want to check you out before granting credit, so be prepared to share information. You might want to put together a few financial details to shorten the wait in the sales manager's office. (He or she will ask for information such as where you bank, whether you rent or own your home, whether you've leased a car previously and whom you leased from, and what your credit rating is.)

a. SHOPPING FOR CREDIT

Just as you shop around for the right car, you should shop around for the financial arrangement that best suits your purposes. Only then do the deal. Compare rates, terms, and bottom line numbers, and you'll be surprised to see how many organizations want to do business with you (if you can demonstrate reasonable creditworthiness, although some lenders even claim to take on any borrower, no matter what tainted credit history he or she brings to the table).

Banks, credit unions, finance companies, auto manufacturers' own financing agencies, car dealers themselves (although they often sell the contract they write with you to other financial institutions), relatives, friends, your own company, and various leasing organizations are all sources of funding.

For the qualified borrower, there is real competition out there to get you into a financial commitment, so you should have a look around for what's available that best matches your needs.

It's a wiser buyer who has the financing angles covered before hitting the showroom floor. Like shopping for a house, it's good to know if you qualify for a mortgage and how far you can go before limiting out. Knowing the amount of money you can borrow will help you stand firm when the salesperson is pushing you to add just one more option to the car you're buying.

The cost of car loans can vary considerably from one lender to the next, so you definitely should contact a few. Deals that might look generous on paper can sometimes be more costly than they seem; read the small print or get your accountant to advise you. Generally, though, it makes sense to borrow from the source offering the lowest interest rates and the most favorable terms. Really quite simple. We've included a scoresheet that you can use to compare what each lender is offering (see Worksheet #2). Comparing to apples to apples will help you make a sound decision of your choice of lender.

1. The cost of credit

If you're puzzled about what borrowing will cost you, ask the dealer to put it in writing. In most places, stating the exact cost of borrowing money is a legal requirement. These days federal, state, and provincial laws throughout Canada and

WORKSHEET #2
RATING THE LENDERS

ITEM	LENDER 1	LENDER 2	LENDER 3
Name of institution	_____	_____	_____
1. Total amount financed	_____	_____	_____
2. Down payment	_____	_____	_____
3. Loan period	_____	_____	_____
4. Annual (interest) percentage rate	_____	_____	_____
5. Monthly payment	_____	_____	_____
TOTAL	_____	_____	_____

Notes

_____

_____

_____

_____

_____

_____

_____

_____

_____

_____

_____

the United States make it almost painless for people to shop for credit. Certain information about loans must be given in writing to the customer before the contract is signed. The finance charges must be stated in terms of actual dollar amounts AND the annual percentage rates shown.

That finance charge expressed as a dollar amount outlines exactly how much you are paying for your loan. It usually includes things such as interest charges, various service fees, and loan insurance, if applicable.

Don't confuse loan insurance with car insurance. Some lending institutions insist that you insure the loan while others are not so fussy. Whatever the requirement, loan insurance is usually worth the small monthly sum involved because, simply stated, if something dreadful happens to you, your family won't have to take over the payments while the car rusts in the driveway.

Dollar amounts are easy to compare if you request information from lenders based on similar time payment periods. Most loans are paid back over 36, 48, or 60 months, with regular monthly payments, but you can often work with a lender to customize a payment plan that's best for you.

If you don't know what length of loan you want, a comparison of annual percentage rates becomes more meaningful. (The cost of credit is usually expressed as a yearly percentage.)

2. Keeping costs down

While nobody can do anything about the prevailing interest rate, there are ways to keep the cost of car loans down. Sometimes an auto dealer will offer special low-interest rates as a buying incentive, but remember that if you take advantage of these deals, there will not be as much flexibility to bargain on the price of the car.

The best way to keep credit costs down is to pay the loan off in the shortest possible time. Choose a three-year term rather than a four- or five-year period. You can also choose to pay the loan off even quicker; opt for a one- or two-year term if you can handle the higher monthly payments.

Longer term loans might seem appealing with their low monthly payments, but costs run high. Also, you might end up paying more than the car is worth at some stage of a particularly long loan period.

Another wise move is to make the largest down payment you can get together and try not to borrow money for the deposit — yes . . . save up for it the good old-fashioned way if you can. Put down one quarter to one third of the car's price and you will find the monthly payments much less arduous come payday. Remember too that "no-money-down" deals from some auto retailers are tied to extra-high interest rates.

If you can, it's a great idea and very, very satisfying to pay off the loan as quickly as possible, even if the contract has some time to run. If a sudden windfall of cash comes your way, use it wisely and pay off this loan. In most cases this will mean a credit refund coming your way. YES!

3. Signing the contract

It's important that you understand the details of the contract you sign when borrowing money. *Always* be sure you know how much money you are ultimately going to pay. Otherwise, a loan is the same as any other contract. Make sure you're not signing your life away. If you have any doubts, ask the person handling the transaction to explain it to you step by step. It's important that you know both your responsibilities *and* those of the lender.

b. SO YOU WANNA *LEASE* A CAR?

If the car you really, really want is a bit too pricy for your finances, there is another way to get it into your driveway.

To lease or to buy? That is the question. And it's a big question facing many people when the time rolls around to think seriously about acquiring a new or used car, van, pickup, or sport utility vehicle. (Yes, *used*! Lease companies will happily lease used vehicles, with certain restrictions based on age, condition, and estimated resale value after the lease expires.)

According to recent studies, one in three North Americans now leases a new vehicle — a surprising figure considering that a decade ago leasing was confined almost entirely to a small section of the business community. Thing was, companies back then leased cars for their management or sales teams (definitely a perk for many and for the firms a tax write-off), and the auto industry realized that this was a great concept for moving a lot more product. Private, not-for-business leasing slowly gained popularity over the years until now it's an option being offered by virtually every dealer (new or used), bank, and finance organization.

While leasing is still considered "the alternative" to traditional auto financing schemes and represents the smaller percentage of deals, it continues to grow quite dramatically, and you should consider what it entails.

1. So what is leasing anyway?

Simply put, a lease plan allows qualified (sorry, you still have to be creditworthy) customers to pay for the portion of the vehicle's life that is used, rather than paying for the entire vehicle, as with conventional financing.

Leasing programs are available from most major automakers and leasing specialists, who offer comparable basic benefits. In addition to low up-front costs and reduced monthly payments, the various leasing plans allow customers to drive "more vehicle for their money" and also enable them to switch to a new model more often. Another important benefit is that you don't have to face resale risks or trade-in trauma.

The low monthly payments can be further reduced if a customer decides to make a larger down payment than is actually required. This is known in the leasing business as "capitalized cost reduction."

Some drivers who opt for leasing use the money saved in monthly payments to add more options to their vehicles — for example, CD players, custom wheels, and towing packages.

If you decide to lease, you should look at including an "option to purchase" clause in your lease contract. When the lease runs out, you could have that important option reading in your favor . . . and you could then buy the car for cash. (As well, many lease companies will be pleased to create a special short-term lease so even that final price can be financed by them.)

If your vehicle is used for business purposes, leasing can offer distinct tax advantages, but you should discuss this with an accountant or tax adviser before signing up.

2. What does leasing cost?

Let's take a look at what a typical lease customer faces when the vehicle under scrutiny costs $20,000. At the end of the lease term the vehicle might be worth, say, $9,000.

If the vehicle was purchased using traditional bank financing, the starting point for determining the down payment and monthly payments would be the entire $20,000. If the same vehicle is leased, monthly payments would be based on $11,000 — the difference between the original cost and the estimated value at the end of the lease period. Consequently, monthly payments are less than they would be if the vehicle was financed in the traditional manner. (For a used car, the same calculations are made, based on the difference between the car's resale value at the start of the lease and the projected resale value and mileage at the end of the lease.)

Lease contracts can be drawn up for a variety of terms: two-, three-, or five-year periods, or even over 12 months. Lease companies can custom design their lease paper to best suit the needs of the customer, so you should outline your requirements when speaking to them. Some leasing arrangements will include the costs of warranties and servicing; under other leases you'll cover these costs out of your own pocket.

Shorter term leasing means that drivers can enjoy a vehicle during its most trouble-free years. Costly replacement of "wear and tear" items such as tires, brakes, and shocks is something the next owner will worry about.

At the end of the lease the customer simply returns the vehicle to the dealership and an evaluation is performed to determine whether excessive wear and use charges are applicable. If the vehicle has been properly maintained and hasn't had its odometer run up to unacceptable levels (lease firms will tell you what figures they consider acceptable when you negotiate the lease), there is no further obligation. The modest security deposit, collected when the deal was originally made, is refunded.

If the customer wants to keep the vehicle, the dealer stands by a guaranteed purchase price written into the lease right from the start. Vehicles *can* be returned before the lease is up, but it's worth remembering that this can be costly — especially during the first half of the lease term.

Lease customers must insure their vehicles just as they would if an outright purchase was made. Some leasing contracts demand specific insurance requirements before a deal can be concluded.

Major auto dealers with leasing and financing schemes available can provide comparisons between the two for a specific vehicle and you should ask for this.

Just as there are many organizations willing to finance the purchase of a new or used car, there are many companies specializing in providing excellent lease programs. Comparison shop with lease companies to establish what's ideal for you. Worksheet #3 allows you to keep track of the different aspects of leasing each company you investigate offers. Use it as a basis for comparison of leasing programs.

Leasing may make it possible for you to drive the hot little sports car or the sleek prestige car that you thought was out of your reach. Keep it in mind as an option when you finally make your trip to ... The Dealership.

WORKSHEET #3
COMPARING LEASING PROGRAMS

ITEM	LEASE CO. A	LEASE CO. B	LEASE CO. C
Name of company			
Total amount leased			
Deposit			
Lease period			
Monthly payment			
Total number of payments			
Cost of lease			
License cost			
Registration cost			
Taxes			
Other fees			
Who maintains?			
Service plan			
Penalty to break lease			
Penalty for excess mileage			
Rebate if less miles driven			
Penalty for default/ late payment			
Wear-'n'-tear-rules			
Renew at lease end			
Buy-back amount required			
Minimum insurance required			

5

NOW WHAT DO YOU DO?

Choosing a dealer

A good sales person: One who sells goods that won't come back to customers who will.

Unknown

Choosing a dealer is simple, right? You just check who has the biggest ads and the cheapest prices in the paper and off you go ...

It should be that straightforward, but in practice ... no way.

For the first-time car buyer, selecting the right dealer is vitally important. After all, you might be beginning a relationship which could last many years — even a lifetime. As a rookie in the car-buying business, you need to find a dealer you can really trust, with whom you feel comfortable, and a company you can rely on throughout the ownership of your first car and perhaps in years to come.

a. SO MANY DEALERS, SO LITTLE TIME

1. Big versus small

Dealerships representing the major manufacturers in large towns or cities, especially if they've been around a long time, are usually very reliable. Chances are they've built up a reputation that they intend to hang on to. Large operations usually have the most up-to-date service facilities with all the latest computerized testing equipment, along with a service staff that is regularly subjected to training sessions with the automaker's technical experts.

There is a lot of competition for both service and sales jobs in a marketplace where downsizing and unemployment threaten, so dealers are able to pick top-notch people from the pool of job applicants. Once picked, staffpeople like the security of a large dealership, so they tend to be there for the long term.

Try to find out if the dealership has experienced an unusually high turnover of salespeople. Some dealerships put a lot of pressure on their sales teams, ruling by fear-of-firing, while others maintain a wonderful atmosphere where professional salespeople just keep getting better with time … and their lucky customers benefit greatly. You might feel better dealing in a happy sales environment.

Big dealerships are not immune to sloppy management and financial woes, though, and some have incentive schemes for salespeople that demand high-pressure tactics — something no first-time auto buyer wants to get involved in. Your local Better Business Bureau or its equivalent can tell you if there have been complaints about a dealership.

Despite the marketing clout of big dealers, smaller operations should certainly not be ignored. They can also be reliable prospects for that first car buy. Small dealerships, sometimes specializing in just one make of car, are often family operations with lengthy histories. The staff are friendly and competent, and it may be easier to maintain a long-term relationship with "your" salesperson because he or she will stick around.

Shop around for your dealer and find a place you feel comfortable.

2. Urban versus rural

If you live in a rural area, a small dealership may be your only choice anyway. And that may be lucky, as rural car dealers

Supremacy
in Fine Steel

In the percentage of Costly Chrome Vanadium Steel used, Dodge Brothers Motor Car outranks any other automobile in the World, regardless of cost.

It is everywhere conceded that Chrome Vanadium Steel is the toughest and most enduring metal ever created for use in the vital parts of a motor car.

It may not be so well known, however, that Dodge Brothers Motor Car ranks *first in the world* in the use of this costly and fatigue-proof material.

Dodge Brothers power assembly is almost entirely Chrome Vanadium—motor, connecting rods, crankshaft, transmission, universal joint, drive shaft, differential and rear axle.

Even the front axle is Chrome Vanadium—

the entire steering unit—and *every* leaf of the springs.

In fact, wherever *any* manufacturer uses alloy steels, Dodge Brothers use costly Chrome Vanadium. And in numerous instances Dodge Brothers employ it where plain carbon steel, even in the costliest cars, is commonly thought sufficient.

This has been true from the day Dodge Brothers built their first motor car.

This explains why the words *Long Life, Safety* and *Dependability* are habitually associated with the name Dodge Brothers wherever motor cars are serving mankind.

DODGE BROTHERS, INC. DETROIT
Dodge Brothers (Canada) Limited
Toronto Ontario

DODGE BROTHERS
MOTOR CARS

with low overheads can sometimes "sharpen their pencils" more and give you a better deal than big city operations that have to cover much higher expenses.

With a lower population base to draw on, these dealers also rely on attracting a few buyers from city or suburban areas. Their enticement is often outstanding prices.

A rural dealership might not place several pages of ads in the local papers, but it is certainly worth investigating.

3. New versus used

Major new car dealerships are often the best source of good used cars. They keep the most clean and reliable trade-ins for their used lot and have first-rate service facilities to prepare these cars for sale. New car dealerships are often able to handle after-sales problems more effectively.

There are some excellent used car specialists around, but they have to be hunted out. Every city seems to have its strip of used car dealers; some are well-established operations with good reputations while others are fly-by-night traders who are often, literally, "here today, gone tomorrow."

It's not easy to judge just what a good used car dealer is. Look for one who's been around awhile. Ask your friends if they've had good experiences with specialized used car dealers, or check with the local Better Business Bureau. Regular ads in local newspapers or magazines may indicate stability.

Since all used cars are sold with some kind of warranty, ask your used car dealer if there is a service shop on the premises or, at least, a solid arrangement with a nearby garage. If something goes wrong with your car during its warranty, will the dealer be able to put it right?

> **Worst bet for a used car**
> Ironically, this is one that's often recommended as a best bet, and that's buying a car that's been in a rental fleet.
>
> It's true that they look very tempting: usually less than a year old, often with as little as 10,000 miles on them. But remember, these cars have taken a lot of abuse in their short lives. They've been driven by dozens if not hundreds of different drivers in ways that those people would never dream of driving their own cars. I've heard too many stories of people taking rental cars drag-racing on dirt roads to ever even think of buying one. And most rental companies do only minimal maintenance: They're interested in quick turnaround, not in long-term staying power.
>
> *~from* Everything Women Always Wanted To Know About Cars *by Lesley Hazleton*

A recent addition to North America's retail auto scene is the "mega used car dealer" with huge selections and extensive service facilities. These dealers will likely prompt smaller operations to provide better after-sales service and might also nudge the more shady used car operators out of business. Not a bad thing.

4. Sales history

It's easy to get your hands on information about how long a particular dealer has been in business. Remember, though, that a long history in the auto sales business is not necessarily a guide to ultimate reliability. New dealerships are often set up with very high standards and top-class staff at huge expense. Good examples of this are the luxury car divisions established in recent years by major Japanese automakers.

These stand-alone chains of dealers have won many awards for sales and service excellence.

5.   Best time to buy

If you're shopping for a new car, there's not much doubt that fall is the best time to buy. Current year models are being sold off as quickly as possible to make room for the upcoming model year's offerings. Savings can be considerable, but watch out for cars that are being totally updated for the next model year. Your "old version" is likely to depreciate more rapidly than it might otherwise have done.

If you do decide on a car that is being phased out, be sure to get a really good deal on it. This may be a good choice if you don't really care about having the latest and greatest. While the all-new version of the car may look different, there may in fact be no practical improvements under its sleek bodywork.

There is not really a best time to buy a used car. While dealer lots are often crammed with trade-ins each fall as new models arrive, the strong used car market of recent years keeps prices high all year round.

Best bet for a used car
One that's just come off a lease. It will be in good shape since leasers face heavy penalties for abnormal wear and tear, and at, say, three years old, it should cost no more than half of its original sticker price. In fact, as more and more cars come off leases, the used-car market will be better than ever before, and you should be able to get great cars, relatively new, at terrific prices.

~*from* Everything Women Always Wanted To Know About Cars *by Lesley Hazleton*

---

b. NARROWING DOWN THE CHOICES

You've decided to buy or lease a new car. You've decided which type of vehicle will be best suited to your needs *and* you've got a handle on the extras or options you would like to load the basic car with, *and* you've got a basic budget figure in mind (with a feeling of how far you can stretch the sides of your pocketbook before they explode.

Now you've zeroed in and visited two or three dealers that carry the kind of car you're thinking about buying. Maybe they're dealers carrying the same manufactured brands, maybe not, but you now have to decide who is going to get your business. How?

Like many other decisions you make, a great deal of your decision about choosing the right dealer will be based on gut feel. Worksheet #4 is simple scoresheet that will help you choose the dealership that will make your car-buying experience a joy now, and with no hangover afterward!

It's easy enough, by the way, to take a stroll through the service department and the service reception area. Ask a couple of customers what their thoughts are. Would they recommend the dealer's service end of the business? People are usually quite willing to talk about their auto servicing experiences, either good or (shudder) bad.

> *Tony: The shiny new Mustang looked great as the saleswoman handed over the keys. I felt pretty good until a mechanic giving the car a final check slammed the hood — right on a tool he'd forgotten to remove. The car was driven straight to the body shop for repairs to the dented hood, and I'd never even driven the darned thing!*

WORKSHEET #4
SCORING THE DEALERS

Rate the dealers on a 1 to 10 score, 1 being at the bottom of the heap, 10 being far ahead of the others — where you want to be!

ITEM	DEALER 1	DEALER 2	DEALER 3
Name of dealer	_____	_____	_____
Is the dealer handy (for follow-up service later)?	_____	_____	_____
Is the dealer's reputation (as you know it) at the top or bottom end of the scale?	_____	_____	_____
How do your friends and family who have used the dealer rate it?	_____	_____	_____
On a walk-thru visit, how do you rate the dealer's "housekeeping" (is it organized? not?)	_____	_____	_____
Interior areas	_____	_____	_____
Outside lot	_____	_____	_____
What are you impressions of the showroom (in appearance)?	_____	_____	_____

WORKSHEET #4 — Continued

ITEM	DEALER 1	DEALER 2	DEALER 3
What are your impressions of the service department (in appearance)?	_____	_____	_____
What were your first impressions about the service people when you asked about maintenance costs?	_____	_____	_____
Were the sales-people friendly?	_____	_____	_____
Knowledgeable?	_____	_____	_____
Genuinely helpful?	_____	_____	_____
Did they show a genuine interest in the car you've got your eye on?	_____	_____	_____
Does the dealer have *exactly* the car you want?	_____	_____	_____
What does your gut feeling tell you? (Before you add up the numbers, which dealer seems best?)	_____	_____	_____

c. WHEN YOU'RE READY TO BUY . . .

It's often said that the driving test is one of the three most traumatic experiences of a person's lifetime — after death of a family member and marriage — but many would argue that their first visit to an auto dealership to buy a car is right up there.

1. Salespeople

For first-timers, a visit to an auto dealership to buy a car can be a daunting experience. The rows of new models on the lot, the glittering facades, the strings of lights, the gleaming showroom floor with even shinier automobiles — all well beyond your budget — and worst of all, the sales staff poised and ready to pounce.

The very notion of being pressured by a guy in a polyester leisure suit, white shoes, and enough gold chains to anchor a cruise ship is among everybody's roster of bad dreams. But the biggest nightmare of all is ending up buying a car you didn't want for a sum way beyond your budget simply because you didn't have the nerve to say "No."

Thankfully, things have changed on the dealership front. While a few old-style "hard sell" salespeople still linger in the retail auto biz like the smell of cheap after-shave, you've got a much better chance of encountering a pleasant, well-groomed, knowledgeable individual who is more likely to give you an unthreatening tour of the automaker's Web site than to "put the arm on you" as soon as you walk through the door.

Good sales trainers don't let new salespeople loose on the showroom floor, but groom them carefully to provide in-depth information and guidance that is important to car buying decision-making. Sales staff also get extensive training from auto manufacturers. Particular attention is being paid to the growing women's market, and major dealerships in large centers usually make sure they have staff members who can speak a variety of languages.

It shouldn't take you long to find out if the salesperson knows cars, or if he or she was selling carpets or long distance telephone services last week. Just ask, "So how long have you been in the car business?" — a simple but important question when it comes time for you to make such a major purchase.

If you do feel uncomfortable with a salesperson, look for another or go somewhere else. You are the customer and have every right to choose where you spend your money. If you pick up even a hint that you're being talked-down-to . . . walk. Remember THE CUSTOMER IS ALWAYS RIGHT and if a dealer gives you the gears or the impression that this old adage doesn't fit into its marketing plans, go look for another.

> *Tony:* I was looking over an Alfa Romeo roadster in a showroom a few years back, and the hovering salesman asked how I liked the styling. I said it was fine but that the top looked ungainly when it was up. He became quite agitated and went so far as to suggest I didn't have an eye for "fine styling." I bought a Volvo from another dealer.

The auto business is highly competitive, so those you speak to MUST be genuinely interested in doing business with you. You can quickly tell if they are. The pros in the business are smart enough to know that if they win you as a customer and keep you happy, not only will you be coming back, but you'll be bringing friends and family and building all kinds of new business for them. Good salespeople will stay in touch from the sale itself through delivery and well afterward. Often they'll send you questionnaires that will help them keep on track. (Manufacturers use these questionnaires to rate the dealerships.)

It's always a good idea to browse through a few brochures and even check out basic mechanical stuff about the makes you're interested in before visiting the dealership. This way, you'll soon find out whether your salesperson really knows the product. You'll also arouse the notion in the salesperson that you just might be someone who knows cars and should not be trifled with when the deal is cut. Another ploy is to take a friendly car nut along with you to help out. Again, you won't be quite so vulnerable to a less-than-scrupulous sales type.

Ask a lot of questions — and get the answers. If the salesperson is evasive, find another one; if you get answers that aren't what you are looking for, maybe you should consider another car. There's nothing worse than shelling out a lot of money, only to find you've bought a car that doesn't fit your lifestyle and requirements.

Make sure you get a proper test drive. A quick run around the block with a salesperson is not good enough at today's car prices. Drive the car over a variety of road conditions, good and bad. If you are buying an expensive car, it is not unreasonable to ask to take it for a weekend.

2. The "closer"

However well you get on with your salesperson, you'll have to bid him or her goodbye and be passed over to the business office when you finally decide what model and equipment you want. At most dealerships, a specialist staffer, the closer, takes over when the sale is all but final.

This is when you sort out the financial details and work out payment terms, leases, or bank draft arrangements. For example, if your bank has arranged a loan for you, the closer will be handed the certified cheque or bank draft.

> **Bruce:** *The best car-buying deal I ever negotiated happened 15 minutes before closing time on the third day of a bad-weather Thanksgiving weekend with a first-time salesman who needed price-cutting approval from a fill-in sales manager ... so they could all get home in time for turkey.*

You can also arrange to insure the car at this stage. Most dealerships have an agreement with a nearby insurance operation that will send a staffer over to set things up so you can drive the car off the lot.

Be forewarned, though, that the closer also has a selling job to do on you. You may be offered all kinds of extras from underbody rustproofing, exterior finish coatings or waxes, extended warranty plans, and other costly add-ons which could add up to several thousand dollars.

Most of these items are worthy enough in their own way, but you must remember that the car business is highly competitive, and dealers often make very little on the vehicle itself. Sometimes more profit can be reaped from these extras than from your new vehicle itself. The best plan is to set a very firm limit on what you plan to spend on your car and stick to it. If extras drive it beyond this point, tell the closer that you've reached your limit.

Some add-ons are of dubious worth anyway. Just about all modern cars are factory rustproofed to a very high degree. Dealer-added underbody coating is often nothing more than an extra coat of sealant you don't really need.

d. CAR BROKERS

Okay. We understand. No matter how prepared you might be (even after reading this book), you're still concerned about meeting your dream car on the showroom floor, face-to-windshield.

There are many reasons why some car buyers use car brokers to put them behind the right steering wheel:

- No time, you travel a lot
- You don't have transportation to get to a car lot and you would hate arriving by cab in case a sales rep saw you coming
- Your negotiating skills are definitely not win-win
- You don't know where to look
- You don't know where to start or what you want, and you're chicken to ask
- You're not sure what's out there
- You have no idea what's a fair price for what you want anyway, and even if you knew, you would have trouble asking for it
- You don't have a best friend, brother, sister, father, mother, or business associate who can direct you to his or her contacts and then tag along for moral support
- You get the heebie-jeebies thinking about that trek across the showroom floor (even worse than going to the dentist)

As so you want to deal through a car broker, a specialist whose business is matching you up with the right deal, the right type of car that best suits your needs at the budget you have to work with. Car brokers, the real ones, that is, are usually individuals who really know their stuff. Their backgrounds vary, of course, but generally they come from somewhere within the automotive industry. They might have been mechanics, sales or lease reps, or individuals who ran fleet operations for their own companies.

Their business is based on what and who they know. They have dealer contacts and are in tune with what's in the local buy-and-sell publications or the daily or weekly classified ads.

When you first make contact with a car broker, don't be afraid to ask about previous customers and check out a few references. Remember that the car broker should be an independent agent, not someone paid a kickback or special commission or finder's fee by a dealer. He or she should quote you a flat fee for his or her services, but given the broker's contacts and negotiating skills, even with this fee in place you should realize a reasonable saving over doing it yourself. A car broker can offer appreciable saving, good-sense advice, and all-round solid service (before, during, and after the sale).

Some brokers have a terrific track record working closely for many years with specific customer groups (often individuals in professional groups such as lawyers, doctors, or teachers). And yes ... some are after a quick buck, so that reference checking we mentioned is definitely in order.

The downside of course — what's missing in all this — is that "love at first sight" feeling you get when you spot exactly (or nearly exactly) the car you've been dreaming of since this year's models arrived "at showrooms everywhere."

e. CAR AUCTIONS

Auto auctions are held regularly in most major cities, but they are not a good place for the auto-buying neophyte to shop.

Cars sold at auction are on display for inspection, but there is no way to test drive them or to make a proper mechanical or body inspection. Doubtful trade-ins at dealerships are often shipped out to the auction lot when it's not worth the dealer's while to refurbish them for sale.

For professionals and car buffs who can sort the buys from the junk by eye and experience, auctions can be a source of wonderful bargains. Amateurs should stay away.

f. ACCELERATING THE INTERNET

Just imagine how tough it would be for you to visit and comparison shop if you lived in a very remote location, in a rural community far from the urban scene and the big-smoke auto malls or the dominated-by-dealership streets.

No neon lights, hot-air balloons, midnight madness sales, or bright white search lights. Just the muted tones of your laptop screen or that high contrast, hand-me-down monitor the kids are letting you use. If you've got a computer handy, now you can accelerate your search on the information freeway. In effect, shop the lots without moving out of sight of your coffee mug or your favorite TV sitcom. But sorry, no free hotdogs, popcorn, or sodas ... unless you get up and head into the kitchen.

Car shoppers with Internet access who are looking around for new or used vehicles will no longer have to make the trek to dealer locations, thanks to a number of companies offering Internet Web sites. Buyers can buy 24 hours a day, at their leisure, without demanding order-takers breathing hotly down their collars.

As many Internet auto shoppers are discovering, with no negotiating to worry about, no hassles or intimidation to concern themselves with, and no dealership open-hours to plan their day around, doing business in the Internet is like a quiet tree-lined street after a two-hour traffic jam in a noon-hour heatwave. Not only can the whole exercise be a pleasurable one, but you could well wind up saving a few thousand dollars in the process.

For example, Auto-By-Tel claims it has already sold thousands of cars to Internet shoppers. At Auto-By-Tel's Web site (*http://www.autobytel.com*), just key the make and model of new vehicle you're looking for and whack "send." Before a couple of days go by, you'll hear from a local dealer with a tighter-than-usual price. Dealers subscribing to this service have agreed to charge customers just a little over factory invoice, so pretty good deals are to be had. You won't find the dealers tough to deal with; although they're keeping prices tight for you, their profit margins remain good, as they're not faced with the usual advertising and sales commission costs. While the big three U.S. manufacturers have offered sites for some time now, soon you'll be able to access virtually anyone selling new or used, or even trading, via the Internet. You can shop via buy-and-sell Web publications that show dozens of deals from private sellers as well as dealer groups.

Information appears on the computer screen with colorful graphics, including all the data you could hope for, coupled with photographs. Color coding is often used to classify vehicles by type, price, and other factors.

Browsers can work their way through each dealer's inventory, find out about special deals, check on service details, and scan new car brochures and technical outlines.

Many of these services also make it possible for buyers to contact the dealer by e-mail or telephone and schedule a test-drive. Whew!

One rainy stay-in day we decided to surf the Internet and see what was what on the subject of buying a car. In the search-engine box titled "What," we simply keyed in the phrase "how to buy a car." In seconds we were informed that the search engine had located 2,083,230 documents on our inquiry. Headings such as Auto Outlet, The Internet AutoSource, Which Car

To Buy, How To Inspect and Buy a Used Car, Fool's School: How to Buy a Car scrolled up the screen.

Minutes later we keyed in "auto buying info" and were advised that 4,695,761 documents were available. Subject heading included Auto Buyer's Choice, Buying Autos, Boats and TVs on the Internet, Auto Online — More Dealer Info, Automotive Videos, Don't Risk Buying a Lemon, A Handy Guide — Financing — Automobile, Auto Sales — Used, Automotive — Buying a New Car, Sales, and so on.

You really only need to remember one access point: *http://www.auto.com*, and that would get you to everything. Another great site is *http://www.findlinks.com/autolinks.html*, which links you to all kind of car-related web pages.

Here is *AutoWeek*'s list of car manufacturer Web sites you can visit for product information and dealer locations.

Acura	*http://www.honda.com*
BMW	*http://www.bmwusa.com*
Cadillac	*http://www.cadillac.com*
Chevrolet	*http://www.chevrolet.com*
Chrysler	*http://www.chryslercars.com*
Dodge	*http://www.4adodge.com*
Ford/Mercury	*http://www.ford.com*
Honda	*http://www.honda.com*
Jaguar	*http://www.jaguarcars.com*
Jeep/Eagle	*http://www.eaglecars.com* *http://www.jeepunpaved.com*
Landrover	*http://www.landrover.com*
Lexus	*http://www.lexususa.com*
Lincoln	*http://www.ford.com*
Mercedes-Benz	*http://www.mercedes-benz.com*

Nissan	*http://www.nissancars.com*
Plymouth	*http://www.plymouthcars.com*
Pontiac	*http://www.pontiac.com*
Saab	*http://www.saabusa.com*
Toyota	*http://www.toyota.com*
Volkswagen	*http://www.vw.com*

g. AND FINALLY — A FEW WORDS ON TRADE-INS

If you are thinking of trading in your previous car to reduce the price of your new purchase, consider advertising it in the local newspaper for a week or two first. There may be a buyer out there who is willing to pay just that much more than the dealer. Bear in mind that the dealer is trying to shave costs at both ends of a trade-in deal; the dealer either won't allow you all that much for the trade-in or won't throw in quite so many extras on your new car.

If you do end up trading in, your local buy-and-sell paper is a good place to check out what kind of money you are likely to get. You may not get as much for your old car if you take advantage of low interest rates, "free" extras, and other incentives. Whether you're trading or selling, check out chapter 8 for tips on how to prep your car to get the best price.

And once you've bought your new car, it doesn't hurt to look ahead to your next car purchase and consider that cars with good service histories fetch more money at trade-in time. Have your car regularly serviced by an appropriate dealer (see chapter 9 on greening your car), keep it clean and tidy (wash your car more frequently if you live in an area where roads are salted in winter), and try to stay away from congested parking lots that promise dents and other minor damage. When you go to trade in or sell your car, those bodywork dings translate into lower prices.

6

"PSST, WANNA BUY MY CAR?"

Buying privately

The buyer needs a hundred eyes, the seller not one.

George Herbert

Millions of cars are advertised privately every year and most of them probably end as happy, win-win deals for all parties concerned. If this is the case, why is the business of buying a car in response to an ad, or over the back fence from your favorite neighbor, a relative, or a friend so fraught with misgivings?

> *Bruce: I remember selling a snappy little red soft-top sports car that a cousin couldn't wait to buy from me. It was clean, had a new paint job, and ran like a top (when everything was tuned, that is), but for my wife and me it was a third car that we really didn't need to insure. As the story goes, in good faith we sold the car to my cousin, who abruptly had problems with it, took it for repairs, and was told the frame was bent, it had been in a major accident, etc... It was years before my cousin, Janice, stopped riding me about it. I'm sure she thinks to this day that she was conned into making the deal!*

For starters, almost anyone who's selling anything loves to emphasize the good points, the better features, and the reasons why "you gotta buy it." It hardly seems logical for the seller to say, "Sorry to have to tell you this, but this little beauty here hasn't always been lookin' so good. Had a little problem after the tree incident … and it's amazing how that red paint really covers over the rust, huh?"

In addition, you might be buying from someone who knows absolutely nothing about the car's true condition and therefore doesn't even know whether he or she is passing on correct information. You are unlikely to get anything resembling a guarantee from a private seller; even if you did, the seller may well have moved on by the time something goes wrong.

In worst-case scenarios, you may buy a car that has been stolen or one that still has a bank lien attached to it. If this happens, you have almost no legal recourse and may very well end up with no car and no money (see section **b.4.**).

Despite these potential hazards, there are countless bargains in the private sale market. If a few cautionary steps are taken during the buying process, there's no reason why you shouldn't drive away happily in your new used car.

a. WHERE TO FIND PRIVATE BUYS

The best sources of private buys are the daily newspapers, community papers, and the buy-and-sell type of tabloid publications that are common in almost all urban areas. Many buy-and-sell publishers have branched out to publish specialized editions that cover sports cars, trucks, recreational vehicles (RVs), antiques, classics … in addition to everyday cars.

You should get your hands on these publications as soon as they appear on the newstands. Once you've got them, get on the telephone quickly. Good buys don't sit around too long. If you start calling buy-and-sell advertisers even a week after the paper comes out, you can bet the best deals are gone …. and you will be left with a selection of questionable merchandise.

These publications are also good for familiarizing you with the prices of the makes and models you've decided to seek out. They'll give you a good feel for what's available so you can enter into a negotiating situation with better information. (At the same time as you're doing this research, check out the wonderful variety of auto magazines available at any newstand for test-drive write-ups and consumer reports of various cars. We've listed some relevant publications in our bibliography.)

Usually you'll end up with a couple of good prospects that are worth checking out "in the metal." When shopping around, it's not a bad idea to ask a friend who knows something about cars to come along with you and help out. Having that moral support when you start wheeling and dealing might move the deal to your price range … it's a psychological advantage at least.

b. CHECKING OUT THE CAR

1. By telephone

When you make initial telephone contact with the seller, ask some basic questions that'll save you making a trip if the car's not what you want. Ask:

- Why is the car for sale?

- How long has it been owned by the seller?

- What is its history (including such areas as maintenance background and problems)?

- How many previous owners have there been?

- Have maintenance records been kept and, if so, are they available?

- Has it ever been involved in an accident? (In some areas, information concerning the car's involvement in an accident *must* be given to you.)

If you're buying a car that comes with a service logbook, check out what the maintenance records show and what regular procedures were taken as part of the service warranty.

In snowbelt regions of the eastern and northern United States and in Canada, salt-laden winter roads can ravage cars. There are laws in place to insure sellers disclose whether a car originates from these areas. If you live in this part of the continent, you should ask questions about the car's paintwork and rusting, and find out if it has been garaged or parked on the street.

2. In person

Once you've decided that a particular car is a serious prospect, arrange an appointment to check it out. Try to organize your visit during daylight hours. You'll be able to notice in the day what you might miss under artificial lighting and, of course, if you take the car for a short demonstration run, you'll be able to see all the buttons, levers, and gauges.

Our comments below on what to look for are summed up in our used car flow chart (see Figure #3), which you might want to photocopy and take along with you whenever you check out a car. We also think it's a good idea to take along someone who has "been there; done that." A friend, parent, mentor, or (lucky you) a mechanic can supply that extra set of eyes when you really need them.

We suggest that you compare three or four cars of the same type and close to the same range of asking price. Focus your attention on these considerations:

- **Tires:** Walk around the car and note all of the tires. Are they all from the same manufacturer? Same model of tire? Same size? How much tread is left and does there appear to be any strange or unusual wear patterns? What do the walls of each tire look like? Have they been painted over and do they appear to be filled in, disguising cracked and well-worn surfaces? Do they look safe?

Peek at the inside surfaces of the tires, those facing each other under the car. What shape are they in? Is it obvious they used to be the outside surfaces, but have been turned around to hide the wear and tear? (While you're there, look for any wet stuff leaking onto those surfaces. It could be brake fluid that shouldn't be there.)

Don't forget the spare tire. Open the trunk and take a look. Is the spare in good shape? Is it mounted on the rim, pumped solid, and ready to roll in an emergency? Are there any dents on the rims? If it's a special "mini-tire" supplied by some manufacturers for short distance use in emergencies, has it been used? And if so, is it still in good enough condition to be used for another emergency? Are the necessary tools for changing tires all available and in place? The jack that was supplied with the car when new? The lever (jack handle) and, if provided, the ground support for the jack itself? (Some manufacturers include a basic toolkit with their cars, so ask if such a kit exists. Some European makes have elementary but useful wrench sets that are handy in a pinch.)

While you're in the trunk, check out its general condition. Does it smell okay? (If not, ask why and what can be done about it.) Lift the carpet and check for rusted and repaired areas.

Glass: Check for scratches, cracks, chips, nicks, and discoloration. Press gently on the sides of the glass surfaces to see that the fit is tight. Note if the rubber seal areas are in reasonable shape or if they are cracked or dried out.

FIGURE #3
USED CAR BUYER'S CHECKLIST

OUTSIDE

Glass

☐ Scratches

☐ Cracks

☐ Fit loose/ tight

☐ Clear view

Tires

☐ All same?

☐ Wear patterns

☐ Good tread?

Lights

☐ Interior

☐ Exterior

☐ Signal

☐ Flashers

☐ Backup

☐ Parking

Body

☐ Overall alignment

☐ Doors, hood, trunk (fit)

☐ Trim (tight)

☐ Dents

☐ Paintwork

☐ Rust

☐ Scratches

☐ Body-filler

INSIDE

Upholstery and other soft areas

☐ APPEARANCE and general condition

☐ CHECK all Interior surfaces (dashboard, Ceiling, doors, carpets)

Trunk

☐ Smells?

☐ Stains?

☐ Rust?

☐ Good Spare?

General

☐ Key turn on

☐ Doors open/close easily?

☐ Knobs/levers and handles all work?

☐ Windows open/close easily?

☐ Instruments: check odometer — allow aprox. 12,000 mi. or 20,000 kms. per year of age

☐ Lights all work? instruments, dash, ceiling, glove box, other

FIGURE #3 — Continued

**What to take
when looking**

☐ Adviser, friend,
parent, or
mechanic

☐ Pencil and paper

☐ Small flashlight

☐ Paper towel

☐ Checkbook

☐ I.D.

Check paperwork

☐ Ownership
registration

☐ Insurance

Under the hood

☐ Oil

☐ Wiring

☐ Radiator

☐ Cleanliness

☐ Belts

☐ Auto transmission

☐ Air filters

☐ Decals/stickers

☐ Fluids

☐ Battery

Notes:

_____

_____

_____

_____

_____

_____

_____

- **Lights:** Get the owner to turn on the engine and operate all lights while you're outside. Check high and low beams, signal lights, backup lights, parking lights, flashers, interior glove compartment lights, vanity mirror lights, and, of course, the main interior ceiling light. Some deluxe models also have lights in the ashtrays, reading lights for back seat passengers, map reading lights, and lights fitted into the side of the door as an alert if the door is left open.

  Of course, the dashboard instrument panel is illuminated with lights and many other areas are back lit for convenience. Each car and model is different in lighting configuration, so you should request that the owner give you a "tour" of the lights.

- **Body:** Kneel in front of the car, 20 to 30 feet away, and check the alignment. Do the front tires line up correctly with the rear tires? Does one side dip toward the ground? Does it seem that the car is "looking straight ahead" but the frame is pointing to the side? Not good. Ask if it's been in an accident if you notice something out of kilter.

  Do all the doors, trunk, and front hood fit snugly? Is the trim loose or tight, rusted, peeling, or discolored? Can you spot any dents? What condition is the paint work in? Are there any areas that might have been repaired, smoothed over, and repainted?

  If the car has a vinyl roof or convertible top, check the color and condition. Is the roof torn or peeling? If it is a convertible, ask how the top goes down and check if "all systems are go." Does it have a plastic or glass rear window, and what is its condition?

- **Inside:** Once you've given a passing grade to the outside of the car (or decided that whatever you've spotted is well worth fixing), it's time to look inside.

Open and close all the doors. Do the handles work properly and do the doors open with relative ease? Note if there appears to be a lot of discoloration or undue wear on the door panels.

Try the windows. Do they move up and down without any sticking or jamming? If the car has a sun roof, does it work properly? Is there evidence of leakage problems?

Once you are right inside, note if there are any strange smells? Has the inside been sprayed with something? If so, why? Is the owner trying to mask a smoked-up interior? Check all surfaces for stains, tears, burn marks, and unusual amounts of wear-and-tear. Pull up the floor carpets. Any rust?

If it's a convertible, look under the top. Is there any light coming through? Does the frame seem to be in good shape?

- **Seats:** Sit on all the seats. Any springs sticking into you? Seats in firm and serviceable shape? Can you easily adjust them to whatever configuration you wish? Do the seats recline? Can you shift them about? If the back rest of the back seat is designed to fold down, can it? If it's a split-back seat style, does it work in all positions? If the back seat is designed to be folded out of the way (in some sports utility vehicles), does it?

  Slide in behind the steering wheel. Adjust the seat controls to a comfortable position. Can you see in all directions easily? Can you read everything on the panel?

- **Behind the wheel:** Check the recorded mileage reading on the odometer; allow approximately 12,000 miles or 20,000 kilometers for each year of age of the car. Ask the seller about it if the reading seems way too high.

Making sure the gears are in neutral, turn the ignition on and note how easily the engine starts up and how smoothly it runs. Is the car shaking? Try the sound system: radio, cassette unit, CD player. Do all the speakers work? Can you separate left side, right side, back, and front? Do all the electronic entertainment features work effectively, or do you have to know a few "owner's tricks" to make things happen?

Do the windshield wipers work in all speed positions: low, medium, fast, and intermittent? Do the washers work? Do the heater, fans, ventilation systems, defoggers, cigarette lighter, clock all work? Can you reach and set them easily? Try the horn.

Put the parking brake on and test if it holds when you try to ease the car into gear and move forward or backward. Can you adjust the exterior mirrors from the driver's seat?

Engine: Find the release lever for the front hood over the engine compartment and open the hood. Does the lever work easily?

Open the engine compartment and, with the engine off, check the radiator. If the engine is cool, remove the radiator cap slowly (best done with a rag over the cap) and note the condition of the water at the top. If it has oily stuff floating on top, it might indicate engine oil seeping from a cracked head or block or perhaps a head gasket problem. If that's the case, head out right away to the next car on your list — unless you have a bundle of emergency cash to pay for what could be very expensive repairs. If the liquid at the top of the radiator looks rusty, or if your finger emerges covered with some thick, gooey deposit, the car might need a new radiator.

The engine area should be reasonably clean: not whistle clean like just off the showroom floor, but not in a condition that indicates oil loss to the engine surface. If it appears that the engine has been steam cleaned, ask why, as this type of cleaning is often done to cleverly hide leak spots.

Check out all the belts, looking for wear and tear, dried and cracked surfaces, and disintegration or shredding. Be sure the belts are firmly installed. A car five years or older will likely need the belts replaced.

Take hold of the fan blades and move them around a bit. If obviously loose, you may need to replace faulty bearings.

Check the date on the battery to see if it came along with the original car. If so, it's likely the electrical systems are functioning without too many problems. Check all wires for cracking and wear and tear. Do they have burn marks? Are they bare? Loose?

Take a look at the air filter. A well-maintained car will have a new or nearly new one. Look for a service center maintenance sticker or decal and check the date of the last service. (Sometimes these decals are not under the hood but on the inside edge of the driver's door or in a log book.). Good upkeep usually means a better used-car deal for you.

Run the engine for a while before checking the oil situation. If the car has been stored in a garage, you might look for any oil staining or pooling under the car. Yup ... that usually means a leak somewhere.

In the engine compartment, locate the dip stick, remove it and wipe it clean; reinsert it and remove it again. Check the oil level. Fresh oil is almost clear, usually a light brown or amber, while oil that's been used in the engine for some time is quite dark, almost black. In older engines the oil tends to darken much more quickly than in new ones, but dirty, black oil usually means lack of attention and maintenance. Oil that is nearly white, gray, or smells of gas usually indicates a problem and you should ask about it or move along.

The test drive: If you've worked your way through the list this far and you're generally pleased with what you have seen, smelled, touched, and heard, you're getting close to decision-making time. You need to try it out now under some realistic driving conditions. A quick drive around the block is usually not enough, so arrange with the owner a reasonable stint behind the wheel. Don't rush the text drive.

The process of the test drive is a combination of "checking and listening." Start by checking the steering. When you steer straight, does the car go straight? When you take your hands off the wheel, does the car pull to one side or wander? (Don't try this on a busy street!) Checking your wheel alignment this way is simple yet can be quite revealing. A problem may be remedied simply by properly inflating the tire or by a more expensive steering linkage or alignment repair.

Once you're running along, lower your window, turn the radio off, and listen. Do you hear the quietly smooth pulse of the engine or a wondrous variety of knocks, bellows, clanks, metallic clicking, pinging, tapping, grinding, wheezing, and groaning? Give the engine a little gas and see how the sound effects keep pace. Do the same sounds persist when the car is running idle? Be forewarned if you can't quickly figure out the source of the sounds. If you love the car for everything else, make sure it's your mechanic who sells you on its ownership joys.

Sound effects extend to the transmission as well. Listen while you shift into gear with a foot on the brake. Do you hear quiet, comfortable noises or clanking clunks? If you hear any scary sounds, check it out with the mechanic ... or forever hold your peace.

3. Mechanical inspection

When you've found a car you're definitely interested in, ask the seller if you can subject the car to an inspection by the local auto club affiliate or perhaps a local garage or service station. Many service stations have excellent repair facilities; if you explain to the owner that you will become a reasonably regular customer (once you're a car owner), and that you'll be needing to find a home for your regular maintenance needs, you should be comfortable that the inspection will help you in your decision-making. This is an inexpensive way of finding out exactly what mechanical shape the car is in. If you are an auto club member, this inspection will not cost very much.

> *Tony: There was a time when the shadier kind of used car dealer would fix a leaking radiator by breaking a raw egg into the filler hole. The leak would be fixed all right — at least until the buyer's check was cashed!*

If the seller refuses to agree to this step, or seems obviously unhappy with your suggestion, move along to the next car on your list.

4. Legal checks

If everything checks out well and the car seems a good buy, make sure the owner is really the owner. YES, . . . is the owner, the person who's selling the car, *really* the owner? Take a good look at the registration papers, or verify the ownership at your local motor vehicle licensing or registration authority.

You should also have your bank or other lender make sure there are no outstanding liens against the car. If the seller still owes money on the car, this should be cleared up before you complete the deal or you might be liable for the balance owing. If you are borrowing money from a bank to buy the car, your bank can often help work things out with the seller and his or her bank.

When everything is settled, remember to purchase insurance and have it with you when you go to pick up the car. In some areas you may also have to put new license plates on the car, so you'll need to organize those as well. Even though you might be driving the car only a couple of blocks to your home, everything must be fully legal.

7

"HER '58 T-BIRD'S WORTH A FORTUNE TODAY!"

Cars as investments

To me, fair friend, you never can be old,/For as you were when first your eye I eyed,/Such seems your beauty still.

William Shakespeare

If there's one thing that upsets a car buyer more than "sticker-price shock," it's depreciation.

Finding out that the new model you set your heart on has jumped in price way beyond your budget is bad enough, but discovering that it will drop thousands of dollars in value after a year or two, or even a couple of grand by the time your first week of ownership rolls by, is a double-whammy that's hard to take.

In a competitive market environment in which last year's models are continually upgraded and replaced, it's tough to root out any automobile that'll hold its value. It's not surprising, then, that increasing numbers of car buyers are taking a serious look at the classic car market to kill off the specter of depreciation.

While everyone dreams of finding a usable classic gathering dust in a barn (like Bruce's Hupmobile) and later selling it at many times its purchase price, most people have more realistic expectations. While it *is* possible to refurbish a run-down classic and sell it years later for an impressive profit, most owners of "collectibles" are happy to leave the horrors of depreciation behind them and enjoy pride of ownership.

We spoke to the owner of a pristine 1957 Thunderbird who described his car as a "rolling retirement plan that I can enjoy whenever I like — much more fun than socking away money in the bank."

Many collectors start modestly with an inexpensive but potentially profitable model. They sell it for a small profit after a minor refurbishing and move on to invest in something a little more elaborate. Buying with care and learning as they go along, many collectors end up with rare automobiles worth hundreds of thousands of dollars. While there are a few wealthy collectors able to buy anything that takes their fancy (like Jay Leno, whose collection is valued in the millions), most owners of valuable classics seem to have started in a modest way. There are plenty of collectors out there who got going with a Morris Minor and ended up with a Bentley.

But even with classics that seem impossible to lose money on, care should be taken. The collectible car business has been something of a minefield in recent years, and many unwary and inexpert speculators have been left with substantial losses — much to the joy of the serious old-car enthusiasts. Thankfully, the classic-buying mania of the late 1980s has settled down and prices have returned to reasonable levels. In fact, there has never been a better time to buy a collectible car — unless you had the foresight to snap up $7,000 Ferraris and $3,000 Jags back in the early 1970s.

a. WHAT IS A COLLECTIBLE CAR, ANYWAY?

The term "collectible car" can mean anything from a priceless rarity to a low-volume current model that experts say will gain value rather than lose it. (Beware, though: some recent models believed by speculators to be certain winners in the appreciation stakes have not proved quite as rewarding as hoped. The current Acura NSX, Dodge Viper, and other exotic sports models fall into this category.)

Since most readers will be looking for a drivable bargain with a reasonable chance of holding its price, we'll not dwell too long on multimillion-dollar Mercedes SSSKs, Bugatti Atlantics, or Ferrari GTOs. There are plenty of bargains to be had from various sources that will quietly appreciate and provide plenty of reliable driving pleasure. A recent list of current bargains with investment potential, published by a U.S. auction house, included a British MGA roadster and a German BMW 635 CSi coupe — both of which can be found, in good shape, at prices in the $10,000 to $20,000 range. Examples in rougher shape can be bought for considerably less by the sharp-eyed buyer.

As you might imagine, you can encounter countless pitfalls when buying an older collectible. Some might look terrific at first glance but on closer inspection turn out to be a mass of thrown-together bodywork repairs, strange mechanical upgrades, and nonstandard components.

If you're thinking about a collectible buy, you should certainly have it examined by a friendly expert mechanic who'll know exactly what to zero-in on. Many books have been written about checking out older cars prior to making any sort of financial commitment, but generally if the car looks too good to be true for the price ... it is.

> **Tony:** *Seeing a Mercedes sedan advertised for sale for a ridiculously low price, a buyer quickly hurried to the stated address and clinched the deal. The woman selling the car had discovered that her husband was holidaying in Las Vegas with a girlfriend. When he called asking her to sell something to raise some quick cash, she advertised his favorite car — at a fifth of its value.*

Once you've found a well-maintained classic in your price range, you'll be happy to know that many insurance companies provide special coverage programs for classic cars that are worth checking into. Aimed at restored or restorable vehicles used for hobby purposes, these schemes usually apply to cars at least 15 years old.

b. WHERE TO FIND COLLECTIBLES

1. Car publications

Browse a larger newsstand for car magazines and you'll be amazed at how many terrific publications are available covering North American, European, and Japanese automakers (see the list in our bibliography). The British magazine *Classic and Sportscar* provides good current information on the availability of most sports models, while U.S. publishers provide a raft of material about the domestic classics.

SILENT AS MOONLIGHT ... a magical Fourth Speed Forward* floats you down the highway effortlessly. A new kind of soundproofing (exclusive with Nash) frees you from road rumble. Wind roar is unnoticeable. A new quietness in travel keeps you relaxed.

WHEN THE *Real Thing* COMES ALONG

THEY SAY there's only one in every man's life ... only one certain girl who ever really mattered.

For it's the way of the world—that the Real Things happen but once.

So we wonder what's going to happen to you when you drive a new Nash ... when you and 3300 pounds of silent steel go flashing off to a pinpoint on the far horizon ...

... when an engine runs, but you don't hear it ... when a "click" of a Fourth Speed Forward* sends you bursting into a new range of exciting performance ... when a wheel in your hands turns light as a feather, and nimble gears seem to read your mind.

... when you *see* people outside fighting the cold, raw wind, while you bask in "Weather Eye"* warmth—in fresh air delivered from next June!

... when ruts and street car tracks skim under you unnoticed ... and no whining wind or road noise tips off your speed.

We predict right now that the first five min-utes in a 1939 Nash will make history in your memory.

And as the milestones go whisking by, you suddenly know why there's a bed built into a Nash ... an oversize gasoline tank behind and an all-revealing windshield in front.

For you're going to go adventuring ... In those far-off places lesser cars could never take you.

You've found the Real Thing—at last!

•   •   •

It's as eager to go as it looks—no garage can hold it! You're going to want it as badly as you did your first bicycle.

It's a wonderful car ... best we've built in 24 years of fine automobiles.

We are as happy as you are about prices—*ten* models next to the lowest.

Any day is a wonderful day in a Nash. *What are you doing now?* Make a change for the better!

Four Sizes of Great Cars, 22 Models ... 10 Priced next to the lowest. Convenient terms on the Nash budget plan. Dealers across Canada. Centrally located parts depots for quick servicing everywhere. See your Nash Dealer. Drive this great car today!

*(*Optional Equipment—Slight Extra Cost)*

PASS BY the gas stations. New Nash-LaFayette engine betters 1938 economy by 10% ... gives you terrific new pick-up from 15 to 50 MPH —in 15 seconds, in *high* gear!

This is the four-Door Sedan, 117-inch Wheelbase, priced down right next to the lowest. Ask your Nash dealer about prices. You will hardly believe your ears.

MAD SPRING WINDS can blow hot and cold ... but inside your Nash it's always the warmth you want! Fresh conditioned air, guarded by the Nash "Weather Eye"* ... frees you from dust, dirt, chilling drafts.

It's that New **NASH**

THE CAR EVERYBODY LIKES

85

Buyers can find interesting old cars advertised almost everywhere, and specialist publications carry classified ads for a variety of makes. A glance through a typical classic car magazine reveals potential bargains ranging from a 1968 Jaguar 420 G "in gleaming black" at $8,000 to a 1949 Buick with a claimed 68,000 "original miles" for $8,200. It's hard to imagine either of these cars could do anything but gain in value if they are well maintained and lovingly cared for.

2. Car clubs

Another good source of reliable collectibles is specialist car clubs. North America has hundreds of them — maybe even thousands. They cater to all tastes in classics, antiques, and exotics, from Alfa Romeos to Chevy trucks, from Lotuses and collector Porsches to Studebakers. Membership in the relevant club is a must for classic car buyers. They are great sources for hard-to-find parts, and the members are bursting with knowledge they will share enthusiastically. Cars purchased from club members can be wonderful bargains because hard-core enthusiasts often put more time into their restoration projects than they can ever hope to win back in terms of cash at sale time.

3. Auctions

Many aspiring collectible car owners have looked to auctions as a source; this can be the best move of all. Classic car auctions are now staged all over North America, though the "blue chip" events are still those at Monterey, California; Scottsdale, Arizona; and Las Vegas, Nevada.

Classic car auctions are not as intimidating as some people imagine, and many first-time attendees come away with real bargains. Often as not, cars are put under the hammer with no reserve price, so some serious bargains are driven away. Prices can range from as little as $3,000 right on up to $200,000 or more.

An auctioneer we spoke to advises would-be buyers to research the cars they're interested in thoroughly before they attend — then spend a lot of time checking out possible buys at the preview of the auction itself. It's also a good idea to set a firm budget before the bidding begins. You don't want to get caught up and find you've mortgaged your home and family to buy a classic Jag.

You may not need to worry about ultrahigh prices, though. Collector car prices have bottomed out and there's never been a better time to buy than now.

It's a win-win situation. You get to buy a vehicle that's tried and true, that gives you a warm fuzzy feeling of pride — and if you take care of it, your pride and joy will last forever and can only increase in value. Often you have no interest in selling your baby, but if sale day ever does comes, you'll make a good return on your investment.

8

SO YOU WANNA *SELL* YOUR CAR!

Prepping for private sale

Nothing astonishes men so much as common sense and plain dealing.

Ralph Waldo Emerson

You've decided to cash in on your refurbished classic. Or it's time to upgrade to a larger car for your growing family. Or you want to exchange the Camaro of your youth for a BMW that's more appropriate to your new position as company VP.

For whatever reasons, you've decided to sell. Now what? Selling a car is like buying a car ... but in reverse. Don't let this confuse you. Basically what you need to know about selling your car is what you *knew* when you were buying.

A little bit of planning will do wonders, and if you stay focused, determine a price that works for you and the customer you're hoping to attract, clean up your car, then aim your promotional efforts in the right direction, you'll be pleasantly surprised how fast you can move your once-upon-a-time dream machine that you wanted so much 'way back then.

a. SETTING A PRICE

A price that works for you should also be a price that attracts a buyer. In fairness, everyone should come out a winner.

Take a serious look through your local newspapers or auto buy-and-sell publications, check prices on the used car lots, ask around, talk to the auto mechanic or service station owner where you've been maintaining your car. You might even try discussing what the trade-in value would be if you were to make an arrangement for a new vehicle at a dealership of your choice. (Isn't this the same process you went through when you were deciding how much to pay for a car you had your eyes on?)

Once you've figured out the ballpark range of prices for cars like yours, you've got to figure out what price you can seriously ask.

Be fair … is your car in top shape? Very clean? Would the buyer need to sink a pile of money into getting it through a safety check?

Think about how much money *you* might have to spend to fix the car up. You don't want to be out of pocket after the sale if you can avoid it (see section **b.**).

Remember, too, when you set a price, the prospective customer will probably want to try and knock a few dollars off your asking price. If you're firm on the amount of money you want, add a few dollars to the price for negotiating purposes.

b. GETTING YOUR CAR IN SHAPE

Unless you're planning to sell on the basis of "as is, where is," where your buyer takes the car the way it is with all its problems, you'll want to put everything you can in the best order possible.

Mechanically speaking, you should have your regular service center take a close look at the car and list everything that should be repaired so you're selling a safe vehicle. Needless to say, your budget, how much money you expect to get for the sale of the car, and how much you need to put into your next car purchase will have a lot to do with how far you get the mechanic to move through the mile-long estimate sheet he or she will put together for you.

Keep in mind that regular servicings will keep your car in shape and cut down on mechanic expenses when you're ready to sell. (Chapter 9 tells how you can keep your car's environmental protection system in shape.)

NEWSPAPER AD
"Great little car, kept under cover,
good price, as-is, where-is."

c. PREPPING FOR THE SALE

When you were shopping for a car, chances are you were attracted to one that looked great. Maybe it was a few years old, but it looked as if someone had taken good care of it. Right? So now you'll need to spend a little time to increase your car's cosmetic appeal …

The best advice we could ever give you is this: The day you buy a car is the day you should think about how it will look at sale time. Look after your car from day one and the effort will translate directly to dollars and cents when it's time to trade up or sell privately. This way, when a hot prospect follows up on your ad and arrives to cast a critical eye over the car, you'll be able to show it off at its best rather than struggle to mask its flaws.

Looking after a car means doing as much work as possible yourself, although professional "detailing" firms often represent money well spent (or well invested?).

1. Washing

Obviously your first move in a good prep or cleanup should be to thoroughly wash the car. Detailing experts (the people who clean cars for a living to look like they just came out of the showroom) will tell you that those automatic car washes on every corner may seem okay for occasional bad weather cleanups, but even one pass through some facilities will scratch paintwork enough for it to need extensive rework. Take a close look at any cab or limo for confirmation of that.

So get out in your driveway with a hose and get started. Wash your car early in the morning if possible, or in the evening . . . not in the hot sun of midday when water spots can dry quickly and mark the finish.

Give the car a good soaking with the hose first to get rid of as much abrasive grime as possible. If you ignore this process and get straight into the soaping, chances are you will simply grind in abrasive materials with the sponge.

Give the area under the fenders (yes, *under*) a thorough hosing to get rid of any salt or other undesirable deposits that have accumulated there. This is particularly important if winter travels have taken you over icy roads treated with salt or other corrosive materials. Summer rain can set severe corrosion in motion if salt deposits are left in place.

Then start soaping. Commercially available car wash products are the safest to use. Some household detergents are harsh enough to remove that wax you spent so much time applying last spring.

Begin at the top of the car and work downward. Use a good-size clean sponge or, better still, one of those sheepskin (or imitation sheepskin) wash mitts that car accessory stores sell.

Wash and rinse glass and roof areas before starting on body sides. This helps eliminate soap streaks that may form during drying. When they are dry, clean your windows with one of the many glass-cleaning products you can find in any supermarket.

Use a soft brush to get at the front grille components, light clusters, and other hard-to-reach corners. Detailers recommend using an old toothbrush to remove wax deposits which may build up around the badges or other decorative details.

Once the washing is done, dry your car before water spots can form. Chamois wash leathers are often chosen for this task, but old bath towels work just fine and are easy to clean with a dump in the laundry tub. Some pros say the imitation chamois cloths are excellent, and an insider we know found that old cloth baby diapers were wonderful (and they're great for polishing, too).

2. Waxing

When your car is completely dry, waxing can begin. Waxing should be carried out at least twice a year and possibly more often, especially if your car has a metallic finish. A good carnuba-based wax is best, but be cautioned: it can be expensive.

Follow the wax manufacturer's instructions for application and be careful to keep wax away from those areas of grained plastic so many cars have these days — it will look bad and is difficult to remove.

Use a soft cloth (yup, the diaper will do fine) to polish the wax after it is dry. Carry out this step in good light so you can see any waxed spots you might have missed.

3. Wheels

Wheels can pose particular problems — especially those complex, cast alloy units that look great but are the devil to keep clean. Best advice on wheels is to keep them clean from the start. Wax them as soon as you pick up your car; this makes removal of grime much easier later.

Many cars, particularly some imports, suffer from unsightly brake dust deposits — especially on front wheels where the brakes do most of their work. Be sure to clean this off.

Use a small, stiff brush on alloy wheels, working into all the little nooks and crannies. Do not use abrasive cleaners on this type of wheel, as they can remove protective coating and set you up for severe corrosion problems.

4. Final exterior touches

When the main body areas are well polished up, take some time to work on the chrome. Nothing looks better than a mirror finish that reflects a potential customer's smiling face back to you!

Another hint for finishing the exterior: buy a little can of black tire paint, easy to apply with a small brush or even an old rag. Your tires may not be new, but they'll sure set off the rest of the car. You can also redefine the letters and numbers on the tire with whitener, available in a crayon stick or as a brush-on liquid at your automotive parts store.

While you're poking around the auto shop (or service station) ask about the cleaning fluid that, when applied to the rubber trim around the windows, produces a like-new appearance.

It's the little details that add up to a great-looking car.

5. Interior cleaning

Now that you've restored the outside of your car to pristine, show-room condition, it's time to turn your attention to the interior.

Most types of cloth upholstery can be cleaned easily with a little mild dishwashing soap and water. Dry them off carefully afterward with a clean, dry towel. Some commercial furniture shampoos do a pretty good job, too.

There's nothing quite like leather upholstery, but it does need extra care. Saddle soap should be applied a couple of times a year to stop hides from drying out and cracking. This is particularly important in the southern United States, but leather upholstery in any car that sits in the hot sunshine can suffer serious damage unless it is well maintained.

Keep interior vinyl and moldings clean by regularly wiping them with a damp sponge. Don't let grunge build up in the first place.

As in your home, grit is the greatest enemy of carpets — it gets into the pile fabric and causes a chafing wear-and-tear action as it's ground in. Carpets should be regularly tackled with a household vacuum cleaner. Most vacuum cleaning units specially designed for cars seem useless; they don't have the power needed for deep-down grit removal.

Pay particular attention to the front instrument panels and areas around the sound system. With a few cotton swabs, a small, soft brush, and a soft polishing rag, you can make this area most appealing.

d. ADVERTISING AND PROMOTION

The purpose of an ad is to attract and hold the attention of your prospect while a selling job is done. There is no magic to creating a good one. Take a look at other car ads and carefully word a piece that you think best promotes your car. Information on age, condition, price, and where it can be seen should all be included. If you can afford it, add a flattering photo.

Check out prices for ads in the classified sections of daily papers, local weekly papers, and papers or magazines that are primarily used for selling used cars (buy-and-sell type).

Often you'll be offered a better dollar deal per ad if you buy space in more than one issue. In a daily paper, a one-week ad will work well, but make sure the placement includes a weekend so you'll catch those potential buyers out cruising on Saturday or Sunday.

You might also wish to promote the sale of your car on the bulletin boards in shopping centers, grocery stores, convenience stores, laundromats, community centers, and other public places.

If you live on a busy street, position your car so as many people as possible can see it. Put FOR SALE signs in the windows, with your telephone number. If you're not on a street that catches much drive-by or walk-by traffic, talk to friends about parking it near their houses, ask your service station if you can display it for a short period, or park it on a busy street and take the bus home. Park it at a shopping center for a day now and then. Let as many people as possible see it.

e. KEEP REPAIR RECORDS HANDY

Be sure to keep receipts for repairs, regular maintenance, and spare parts over the history of your ownership, and have them ready to show potential buyers. This lets them know the care and attention you've paid to the car and is reassurance that they'll be buying a well-maintained vehicle. If you have these records, your ad can say, "Full maintenance records available."

f. OWNERSHIP PAPERS

Be sure you know what must be done to transfer ownership legally. This procedure varies considerably throughout North America. Check with the auto registration authorities and your insurance agent, and prepare all the documentation necessary to make a deal. Remember, once a prospect decides that your car is the one he or she wants … you must be ready to make a deal, then get the deal done!

g. MAKING A DEAL ... WHEELING AND DEALING

Wheeling and dealing is really quite easy ... you don't have to sell your car for anything less than you want, and if you've given yourself some room in your asking price, you can move to where you need to be. On the other hand, if you've priced your vehicle fairly, you shouldn't have to cut the daylights out of your asking price to make a sale.

When you meet a prospect, remember that something about the ad you placed or the appearance of the car attracted his or her attention. Try to understand what this prospect is looking for, and promote the benefits of your car that best suit the needs you've just heard about.

Not all prospects will immediately jump at the deal and offer cash on the spot. Don't be afraid to "ask for the order." Say something like, "This car seems to suit your purposes very well ... shall I get the papcrwork going?"

Think about the many ways prospects will want to construct a deal: cash? check? certified check? Decide what you are ready to accept. Do not let the buyer take the car under any circumstances until you're fully satisfied that the money is in your hands or the cheque has cleared and the funds are in your account.

And then you're ready to start the whole process again!

9
"CAN I HAVE THAT IN GREEN PLEASE?"

Environmentally friendly cars

Cars: the first sight that strikes you in any large American city.

Unknown

Drivers don't need to shop around for environmentally friendly cars. Every new car in the North American marketplace has to meet the federal government's high environmental standards, and further research and improvements are happening all the time. (If you want to go really green, there are also zero emission electric cars, which you can read about in section **c**.)

It's to your advantage to keep your car's anti-pollution equipment in working order. Regular servicings ensure that your car is environmentally friendly, that it will meet emission standards and be easy to sell or trade in when that time comes, and that it will achieve peak gas mileage.

We'll tell you how to keep everything running properly, but first a little history and some explanation of what all those wires and gadgets under your hood are for.

a. TAILPIPE EMISSIONS AND FUEL ECONOMY

The problem of tailpipe emissions has been challenging automakers since the early 1970s when legislators first decided that pollution from automobile congestion was making many cities around the world almost unlivable. At that time, vehicle engines weren't too efficient at burning fuel. Internal combustion produced a mixture of toxic gases — hydrocarbons (unburned and partly burned fuels), oxides of nitrogen, and carbon monoxide — which emerged from the average vehicle's tailpipe. All three groups of gases are harmful to human health, and in some cases, to plant life.

The auto industry has spent billions of dollars to cut tailpipe emissions — not always with the prompting of federal legislators. An industry has been developed around auto pollution control over the past two decades and research has produced some dramatic results.

If you're concerned that buying a car with all the environmental goodies might hurt the get-up-and-go performance you were hoping for, don't worry. Back in the 1970s, cars with pollution control systems paid a substantial performance penalty, but that's not the case today. Even modestly powered four-cylinder economy hatchbacks boast full emission control equipment, excellent fuel economy, and performance levels that would shame a sports car of the 1970s or 1980s, thanks to highly sophisticated engine management computers.

These computers — and just about every car, van, and truck has one now — monitor every aspect of engine performance. Fuel is metered to the engine more precisely than ever before, and wastage is kept to an absolute minimum. Harmful emissions that *do* escape the internal combustion process are dealt with by a catalytic converter, located in the vehicle's exhaust system.

Tony: *One indication of the technical complexity of today's engine management computers is that Michael Schumacher's Formula One 1995 world championship-winning, Ford-powered Benetton race car used a "black box" almost identical to the one you'll get in your new Ford Contour or Mercury Mystique. Fuel* *economy is not something most people normally associate with Grand Prix cars, but the loss of a half gallon or liter or so of fuel at that level of racing can be a million-dollar blunder.*

Fuel suppliers have made a contribution too. After all, the bottom line is saving fuel. If fuel is used as sparingly as possible, the environment benefits accordingly. Today's gasolines burn cleaner than ever in addition to providing enhanced performance and improved economy. Steps have been taken by the designers of that pump you use at the gas station to make sure that harmful evaporative emissions are prevented.

According to the Motor Vehicle Manufacturer's Association (MVMA), emissions from today's cars are reduced by 90% on average from uncontrolled levels. Hydrocarbon and carbon dioxide emissions are reduced 96% from the precontrol era while oxides of nitrogen are down by 76% on post-1988 vehicles. The MVMA says that member companies General Motors, Ford, and Chrysler have volunteered to phase in further emission reductions on a regular basis.

Most manufacturers agree that there is still work to be done. Progress continues in the emission control field with the aim of making internal combustion engines as clean as they can possibly be, while still providing efficient transportation.

b. SO WHAT CAN YOU DO?

One quick peek under the hood of any car manufactured over the past few years is usually enough to convince you that maintenance is something best left to a mechanical wizard. Much of this organized "clutter" packed over and around the engine is associated with electronics and pollution control equipment, and it's strictly "hands off" for the amateur backyard mechanic.

So is there anything a green motorist can do to reduce pollution? Yup! Plenty. You can keep your car in shape to reduce harmful emissions and run at its fuel-efficient best. And you can quit dumping tires and batteries at the local junkyard or pouring oil and other engine fluids into the gutter or down the drain.

Whatever small maintenance jobs you are able to perform yourself, however, it is usually the service operation which carries the bulk of environmental responsibility. It's a good idea to use a shop approved by the American Automobile Association (AAA) or the Canadian Automobile Association (CAA). The AAA/CAA sign assures you that the shop follows federal and local environmental rules for repairs and waste disposal, and these facilities are inspected periodically by trained staff to make sure they maintain standards set by their respective governments.

1. The engine

Used cars should have the appropriate computerized engine management systems and exhaust catalytic converters in place. If you're not sure what to look for, have a mechanic inspect the car to be sure that all systems are in place and nothing has been removed or tampered with. Tests carried out by federal agencies have determined that 22% of vehicles inspected had at least one emissions component that was missing, damaged, or in some state of disrepair. When these shortcomings are corrected, hydrocarbon emissions drop as much as 12%.

Environmentally responsible motorists can support the technology by taking their cars in for regular servicing and by using the fuel recommended by the manufacturer. That complex emission control equipment will not work well in a poorly tuned vehicle. All vehicle owner's manuals contain details of service intervals — longer these days than they used to be, thank goodness! It's a good idea to make use of an approved dealer who is likely to have test equipment specially designed for your vehicle. Or at least be sure that your local service station has the right equipment on their premises to get the job done.

2. Tires

No car will maintain its fuel economy potential if it's running on tires that are not up to recommended pressure. According to one source, 70% of vehicle tires are underinflated, affecting fuel consumption by as much as 1% for each pound (just less than half a kilogram) of air pressure under the makers' recommended rating. Underinflation also increases tire wear, contributing to other environmental problems — namely, the mounds of discarded tires in landfills and the increased production of new tires, using more resources, power, etc. You can reduce running costs significantly by extending the life of your car's tires.

Several manufacturers have recently developed tires with tread patterns that lower rolling resistance, enhancing fuel economy and making an environmental contribution of their own.

3. Getting rid of oil and other fluids

Correct disposal of oils and other fluids is important. Oil is more toxic than it might appear and should never be disposed of down the drain or into the ground. Many gas stations now take used motor oil for recycling; it's a good idea to look for one of these stations if you change your own oil.

If all your maintenance is handled by a service station, make sure that its fluid disposal techniques are up to date. Some states and provinces now have specialized businesses that take used oil and filters from service shops and properly recycle or dispose of them. Solvents used by shops for parts cleaning and other duties also need special handling.

4. Batteries

We found the best bet is to purchase a new battery at a place that takes in your old one for proper disposal. Auto batteries have always presented a distinct set of problems because they contain highly corrosive acids. Check your local laws to find out what you should do with dead batteries.

5. CFCs in air conditioners

The air-conditioning systems in many older cars contained a refrigerant that uses chlorofluorcarbons (CFCs), considered by many scientists to be harmful to the ozone layer. Careful handling of CFCs is a must, and most of the bigger shops have specialized equipment to deal with CFC disposal. Better still, most new cars are coming onto the market with an environmentally safe refrigerant.

c. ELECTRIC VEHICLES

Some North American legislators have their sights set on even cleaner vehicles — ones with ZERO emission. Zero emission vehicles (ZEVs) would create no direct pollution at all.

Right now, ZEV means electric car. The state of California has set a deadline for a certain percentage of all vehicles sold in the state to be ZEVs, but electric car development is still at an early stage as far as feasibility goes. The ZEVs we've driven range from practical to no better than glorified golf carts.

The main problem is battery technology. Almost all electric vehicles use large, heavy batteries, and none of them provides anything like the range and performance of a gasoline-powered car. Electric vehicles generally can't go much farther than 62 miles (100 kilometers) on a charged battery. Use the heater, lights, or air-conditioner, and this range drops dramatically.

Where battery technology has advanced to the stage where charging is fast and range and performance acceptable, the charging process takes a large bite of power from the electrical supply grid. In such cases, the environmental burden is simply being switched from one sector to another. There's little point in filling the streets with electric vehicles if more power dams or nuclear generating stations must be built to serve them.

But despite setbacks, most of the world's major automakers have developed at least one electric vehicle, and some have launched production units. At a recent Detroit launch, one manufacturer showed its proposed electric minivan right alongside the gas-powered versions.

> *Tony: Electric cars have a longer history than most people realize. In the early days of motoring, electricity rivalled gasoline and steam as a power source for cars, and between 1897 and 1939 there were no fewer than 565 different makes using this form of motive power. Most of the makers, however, went broke before they'd built more than a dozen cars. Electric cabs were quite popular in London, England, at the turn of the century, but they were too slow to compete with horse-drawn hansom cabs.*

Electric cars probably will become more viable as the years go by. After all, we are running out of oil. As ZEVs show up in dealers' showrooms, expect their range and performance to be very limited and their price to be high. Wealthy motorists with green inclinations will likely be the first to purchase electric cars. A suggested tailpipe emission premium — a polluter-pay concept to discourage the use of inefficient and "dirty" vehicles — may make the cost of ZEVs more attractive.

Even as work progresses on ZEVs, however, many auto industry engineering and research people continue to work on refining and cleaning up the good old internal combustion engine to even higher levels, spending billions on the quest for cleaner conventional powerplants and cleaner fuels.

10
CAR-BUYING CHECKLIST

The car is man's most successful effort to produce the mule.

Unknown

Everyone knows the old adage about a car being the second most costly and important purchase a person makes in life next to a house. Few would argue with this line of thought, but it's also worth considering that, for many people, a car purchase can be even more vexing than signing the deal on a home.

Buying a new or used car doesn't have to be traumatic if a few basic rules are followed. Keep some of these factors in mind and that intimidating salesperson with a flashy suit and engaging smile will not stand in the way of your getting exactly the car you want.

STUDY THE AUTOMOTIVE PRESS: Many magazines publish test summaries of various new models. These are worth studying if they cover the class of vehicle you are interested in. Auto enthusiast magazines are available at newsstands and are well worth perusal even before you visit a dealer. There are also several worthwhile "annuals" that cover every car, van, and truck marketed in North America.

SHOP AROUND: Don't be persuaded to buy the first model you take a shine to. Visit as many dealers as possible in your area and check out every model that competes with the one you have in the back of your mind — new or used. Try not to establish a preconceived idea of what model you want. List your basic needs and price range and keep an open

Test it on
ROUGH ROADS

Test it on
THE HIGHWAY

Test it for
SMOOTHNESS

Test it for PICK-UP

Test it for
VALUE

Tune in "Canada on Parade"—a contribution to Canadian Progress— over radio stations from coast to coast every Friday evening, beginning April 10.

PRICED FROM
$1085
at Factory, Oshawa, Taxes Extra

THE NEW
OLDSMOBILE
A GENERAL MOTORS VALUE

OE3-3

mind. You may find exactly what you need at a dealership or from a manufacturer you never considered.

> *Tony: The first new car I ever "bought" was stolen off the lot and trashed by vandals the day before I was to pick it up. I chose a different model and it proved a much wiser decision, but I never did get to thank the vandals.*

LOCATION: Out-of-town dealers often have lower over-heads than city operations and can therefore "sharpen their pencils" more. With a lower population base to draw on, they often rely on attracting a few buyers from city or suburban areas. Call around and check city versus country prices — you could save a bundle.

WHEN BUYING USED: Consider that major new car dealers are often the best source for a good used deal. They have first-rate service facilities to prepare used cars and also handle after-sales problems more effectively. Large dealers usually ship all the junkers traded in to auction sales or wreckers' yards, keeping only clean, reliable cars for the used lot. There are some excellent used car specialists around, but they have to be hunted out. Advice from a friend is often worthwhile here.

IF YOU BUY A USED CAR PRIVATELY: Use the test service offered by your local automobile association to check it out. Even if you have two or three cars tested before you buy, you could save yourself a lot of cash in the long term. If a seller refuses to subject the car to a test, the chances are he or she has something to hide.

CONCERNED ABOUT FINANCING? Remember that competition is fierce among banks and financial institutions for car loans. Shop around just like you did for the car — you could get a pleasant surprise.

MAKE SURE YOU GET A PROPER TEST DRIVE: A quick run around the block with a salesperson is not good enough at today's car prices. Drive the car over a variety of road conditions, good and bad. If you are buying an expensive, up-market car it is not unreasonable to ask to take it for a weekend.

So I sez to the salesman..."Lemme take 'er for a spin.
See what she'll do...how it handles." And he sez...
"O.K. just around the block, see you in five!"

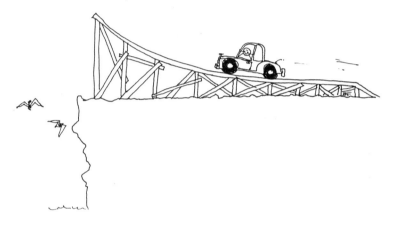

PLANNING TO TRADE YOUR USED CAR? Try advertising it in the local newspaper for a week or two first. There may be a buyer out there who is willing to pay just that much more than the dealer who is trying to shave costs at both ends of a trade-in deal. Remember what we said about automobile association checkovers? Such an offer can speed up a sale and get you the best price.

WHEN YOU TRADE IN YOUR CAR: Remember that if you take advantage of low interest rates, "free" extras, and other incentives, you may not get quite as much for your old car. Similarly, if a dealer offers a low-cost loan, do not expect to be able to "deal" on the price of that new car.

CHECK OUT THE WARRANTY BEFORE YOU BUY: There is very intense competition between automakers right now on the warranty front. Some manufacturers are offering amazing warranty deals and in most cases the customer is the ultimate winner.

WORRIED ABOUT MAINTENANCE COSTS? Take a walk around to the parts counter and check the price of a few typical parts — alternator, water pump, brake parts, and the like. You could get quite a shock and may want to look at other manufacturer's models. In the excitement of buying a new car, this is often forgotten, but it could save a lot of cash when something goes wrong.

SO YOU FINALLY TOOK THE PLUNGE? It's worth considering that cars with good service histories fetch more money at trade-in time. Have your car regularly serviced by an appropriate dealer, keep it clean and tidy, and try to stay away from congested parking lots that promise dents and other minor damage. When you go to trade in your car, those body work dings translate into lower prices.

11
SO WANNA BUY A CAR YET?

Liberty, perfect liberty, to think, feel, do just as one pleases.
William Hazlitt

Now that you're this far along in your research …

- You're armed and dangerous with info overload, know what you want in a car, and ready to take on the local dealers.

- You've decided to hang on to what you have — to make do for just "a little longer."

- You're circling telephone numbers in the local want ads, then dialling to save dollars.

- You're getting set to cruise the used car lots with a friend.

- You're about to access the Internet and see what can be done "sight unseen."

- You're ready to put your own car up for sale, get the best price possible, then get on with reversing the whole process.

But no matter what, you're better prepared than you were reading our introductory comments many pages ago.

The whole thing about buying a car is to be prepared. It doesn't make good sense for you to arrive at the dealership, the private seller's driveway, or the leasing rep's office without first knowing what your needs are, what your budget will stand, and what kind of circumstances you'll be getting yourself involved in.

People have been falling into love/hate relationships with the auto since before Henry Ford's production line got rolling, and you'd think that it would be pretty straight-forward to deal with car buying by this time in automotive history. But things are always changing.

As we were writing this book, we daily spotted differ-ences from the old times in how cars were bought and sold (surfing the net), how the auto marketplace was undergoing radical change (new 1,000-car auto supermarkets), and how financial institutions, too, were constantly adapting their lending practices just to keep pace. We could never say, "Well, that's it. The book's over. Nothing more to write," because every day we'd hear about something new. The car itself is something that's constantly changing. As next year's models appear on the lot today, designers are working on prototypes that will be for sale five years from now.

Although we can pass on some valuable tips to help along the way, ultimately you will be faced with the "Should I do it?" question, and the choice will be yours alone to make.

But there really isn't much to compare with being in the driver's seat of your own car for that first drive.

You adjust the seat position and buckle the seat belts, check the mirrors, turn on the ignition. Preset a couple of your favorite radio stations (or stack a handful of tapes or CDs on the seat beside you), check the sound levels and back seat speaker balance.

Scoping all directions, you release the parking brake, shift into drive or first gear, and off you go ...

- to the bank for new checkbooks,
- to your insurance agent's to arrange extra coverage,
- to the tire store,

- to the battery place,
- to the muffler emporium,
- to pick up seat covers …

and the beat from your V-8 or whatever's hiding in the engine compartment just keeps on going.

APPENDIX

MANUFACTURERS' TELEPHONE NUMBERS

For information on specific makes or models, call the manufacturers direct. They'll send details on products and let you know where their nearest dealer is located.

Acura: 800-862-2872

Audi: 800-822-2834

BMW: 800-831-1117

Buick: 800-521-7300

Cadillac: 800-458-8006

Chevrolet: 800-222-1020

Chrysler: 800-992-1997

Dodge: 800-992-1997

Eagle: 800-992-1997

Ford: 800-392-3673

Geo: 800-2221020

GMC: 800-462-8782

Honda: 800-783-3171

Hyundai: 800-633-5151

Infiniti: 800-662-6200

Isuzu: 310-699-0500

Jaguar: 800-544-4767

Jeep: 800-992-1997

Lexus: 800-872-5398

Lincoln: 800-392-3673

Mazda: 800-222-5500

Mercedes-Benz: 800-222-0100

Mercury: 800-392-3673

Mitsubishi: 800-222-0037

Nissan: 800-647-7261

Oldsmobile: 800-442-6537

Plymouth: 800-992-1997

Pontiac: 800-762-2737

Saab: 800-955-9007

Saturn: 800-553-6000

Subaru: 800-782-2783

Suzuki: 714-996-7040

Toyota: 800-331-4331

Volkswagen: 800-822-8987

Volvo: 800-458-1552

SELECTED BIBLIOGRAPHY

MONTHLY NEWSSTAND AUTO MAGAZINES

These magazines carry road tests and previews of new models in each issue and some publish annual guides to the auto market.

Automobile (U.S.)

Car (U.K.)

Car and Driver (U.S.)

Carguide (Canada)

Classic & Sportscar (U.K. — on classic cars)

Le Monde de L'Auto (French)

Motor Trend (U.S.)

Road and Track (U.S.)

World of Wheels (Canada)

WEEKLY NEWSSTAND AUTO MAGAZINES

Like the monthlies, these publications carry road tests and new model information. *Auto Motor und Sport* prints details of models destined for North America well before U.S. or Canadian magazines.

Auto Motor und Sport (Germany)

AutoWeek (U.S.)

CONSUMER MAGAZINES FEATURING AUTOMOBILES

These publications carry regular reports on new cars and other automotive products. Some feature special auto issues or annual model round-ups.

Consumer Guide

Consumer Reports

Popular Mechanics

Practical Mechanics

ANNUAL REFERENCE BOOKS

AutoIntelligence New Car Decision Maker (Katzka and Yankus)

Consumer Reports New Car Buying Guide

Le Guide de L'Auto (Jacques Duval and Denis Duquet, French)

Lemon-Aid New Car Guide (Phil Edmonston)

Lemon-Aid Used Car Guide (Phil Edmonston)

GENERAL REFERENCE BOOKS

A Consumers' Guide to Automobile Leasing (Mike Burke)

Everything Women Always Wanted To Know About Cars (But Didn't Know Who To Ask) (Lesley Hazleton)

TV SHOWS

These network shows evaluate new models and feature segments on a wide range of automotive topics.

Driver's Seat (Canada)

Motoring 97 (Canada)

MotorWeek (U.S.)

FINANCIAL FREEDOM ON $5 A DAY

A step-by-step strategy for small investors

Chuck Chakrapani

$10.95

Even if you know nothing about investing, this book will show you how to achieve financial freedom starting with very little money. It explains how you can use investment strategies that most people think are available only to the rich. Also included is a valuable resource directory that gives the names and addresses of important contacts throughout North America.

This enlightening book starts from square one, giving readers the know-how and the confidence to start making small investments. From there, readers are led step-by-step through the investment process, from making small investments to the most prudent ways to diversify.

Contents include:

- How to start your investment program even if you are an absolute beginner
- How to save money painlessly, even if you do not have any savings at the moment
- Investment opportunities available to the small investor
- How to take advantage of profit opportunities even if you have just $100 to invest
- How to get free information on different investments
- How to keep yourself informed about current developments

UNDERSTANDING AND MANAGING FINANCIAL INFORMATION

The non-financial manager's guide

Michael M. Coltman

$9.95

Many small business people are frightened by the prospect of balancing ledgers, drawing up income statements and balance sheets, and comparing their current assets to their liabilities. However, this book takes the mystery out of accounting. In easy-to-understand language, this book takes you through the "after the basics" accounting procedure for the small business.

Contents include:

- An overview of accounting
- Financial statements
- Depreciation
- Income statement analysis
- Balance sheet analysis
- Internal control
- Cost management
- Fixed and variable costs
- Cost-volume-profit analysis
- Budgeting
- Cash management

A SMALL BUSINESS GUIDE TO DOING BIG BUSINESS ON THE INTERNET

by Brian Hurley and Peter Birkwood

$14.95

Designed specifically for the entrepreneur, this unique book shows readers how to take advantage of the Internet's huge potential and how to set up an Internet-based business. It thoroughly analyzes the Internet's exciting opportunities, which can be used to form a new business or enhance an existing one. Key elements relating to starting a business on the Internet are provided, including:

- The necessary hardware and software required to obtain Internet access
- Using the Internet toolbox
- Surfing and finding things on the Internet
- Determining whether a current business has Internet potential
- Security and legal issues involved
- Non-traditional business opportunities available on the Internet
- Selecting an Internet service provider that will work best for your business
- A look at what the future holds for the Internet

ORDER FORM

All prices are subject to change without notice. Books are available in book, department, and stationery stores. If you cannot buy the book through a store, please use this order form. (Please print)

Name_____

Address_____

_____

Charge to: ❑Visa   ❑ MasterCard

    Account Number_____

    Validation Date _____

    Expiry Date_____

    Signature_____

❑**Check here for a free catalogue.**

YES, please send me:

_____ **Financial Freedom on $5 a Day**

_____ **Understanding and Managing Financial Information**

_____ **A Small Business Guide to Doing Big Business on the Internet**

Please add $3.00 for postage & handling.
Canadian residents, please add 7% GST to your order.
WA residents, please add 7.8% sales tax.

Please send your order to the nearest location:

IN CANADA
Self-Counsel Press
1481 Charlotte Road
North Vancouver, B. C.
V7J 1H1

Self-Counsel Press
4 Bram Court
Brampton, Ontario
L6W 3R6

IN THE U.S.A.
Self-Counsel Press Inc.
1704 N. State Street
Bellingham, WA 98225

Visit our Internet Web Site at: http://www.self-counsel.com/